THE TY COBB EDUCATIONAL FOUNDATION

Through Fifty Years

By Jerry Atkins

with a Foreword by
Harry Downs
and an Afterword by
Loran Smith

Published by
FIVE POINTS PRESS
550½ Milledge Circle
Athens, GA
706-534-9270

Printed in the United States of America
1st Printing, 2007

Cataloging-in-Publication data for this book is available from the Library of Congress.

ISBN 978-0-9789539-0-4

Book and jacket design by Thomas R. Bledsoe

TABLE OF CONTENTS

This Book is Dedicated to

Rosie Atkins

Perhaps "The Georgia Peach" was not a well-liked man in his lifetime, but his dream of "doing something along educational lines" has provided many a smile on the faces of numerous Georgia students through the years.

It has been a great pleasure to make an attempt to capture the heartbeat of the Ty Cobb Educational Foundation through its first 50 years.

It would not have been possible without my wife, Rosie, who has taken pride in helping the Foundation reach goals far beyond what Ty Cobb could have possibly imagined.

My introduction to the Ty Cobb Educational Foundation came in 1977 when Dr. Harry Downs, my boss and president of Clayton Junior College (CJC), was named to the Board of Trustees. As Director of Public Information at CJC (now Clayton College and State University), I designed the brochure used to recruit applicants for Ty Cobb scholarships.

My association changed in 1981 when Dan Hardage, a member of our faculty, was named Secretary to the Foundation, replacing Carroll McMahon who had held the position for 25 years. Dan met an untimely death later that year, and my connection to the Foundation was to take yet another major turn.

Rosie took the reigns as secretary in January 1982 and remained in the position for 22 years.

During that time, through her expert computer skills, I saw her turn the Ty Cobb Educational Foundation into a finely tuned operation. An expert typist, she bought an expensive electronic typewriter in the early years to pound out the numerous letters to scholarship hopefuls and recipients.

Then, as the numbers increased, thank goodness for the computer! Rosie converted the files to computer-generated records and documents. She designed her own programs to fit the "animal" that she created and smoothed them out as the years went by.

I watched it all with amazement, read letters and heard the many stories of student applicants, and enjoyed the association with one of baseball's greatest stars. I regret that Ty Cobb isn't here today to see what he started.

I became a part of the Ty Cobb Educational Foundation through the years, and it's with a great deal of sadness that we hand off these duties to someone else. It's been a lot of work, but it's also been fun...it's been a good ride.

And, I owe it all to Rosie!

FOREWORD

By Harry S. Downs

Ty Cobb joined the Detroit Tigers in 1905 at the age of 18. Upon retirement in 1928, he held 90 major league records. Some of those records still stand today. He was among the initial five to be inducted into major league baseball's Hall of Fame with the highest vote of 98.23%.

He was also a very astute and successful businessman. As a philanthropist, he was surely the most charitable of all professional athletes.

In 1959 he gave funds to his hometown of Royston, Georgia, to construct a hospital, Cobb Memorial Hospital, in loving memory of his mother and father. Today, this initial hospital has grown and developed into a health care system that serves several northeast Georgia counties; the system comprises two hospitals containing 150 beds, three long-term health care facilities with 353 beds, an assisted living facility, a home medical equipment service, and a full-service rehabilitation center for adult health care and pediatrics. In 1998, the health care system opened the world-class Ty Cobb Museum, also located in Royston.

In 1953, Mr. Cobb established the Ty Cobb Educational Foundation for the sole purpose of providing scholarships for Georgia residents who could not otherwise afford to attend college. It has been my great honor and pleasure to serve as a member of this scholarship board since 1977.

The first scholarships awarded by the board were to six students in the total amount of $2,800 during the 1954-1955 academic year. Over the course of these 50 years, the foundation has awarded more than nine million dollars to 6,500 students. During 1997 through 2003, more than one-half million dollars was awarded each year.

The success of the Foundation and its contribution toward educating our Georgia citizens is truly remarkable. I am sure that Mr. Cobb would never have dreamed his foundation would touch so many lives in such a meaningful way.

The positive work of the Foundation is greatly enhanced by the cooperating institutions of higher education, particularly their financial aid officers, by the extraordinary service of Carroll McMahon and Rosie Atkins, who served as secretaries through these many years, and by a succession of dedicated Board members.

Our unending gratitude is conveyed to Jerry Atkins for his time and extraordinary talent in researching and writing this account of the first 50 years of the life of the Foundation.

INTRODUCTION

by Jerry Atkins

The only time I saw Ty lose control of himself was when some of the kids he had put through school came around to thank him. They broke into tears and Cobb cried along with them.

–George Maines, a longtime friend, speaking of Tyrus Raymond Cobb

If Tyrus Raymond Cobb were alive today, he would be 117 years old and looking forward to 118. Born on December 18, 1886, Cobb didn't make it into the 21st century, having died of cancer and other complications on July 17, 1961, 43 years ago at this writing in the year 2004.

A native of Royston, Georgia, Ty Cobb may have been baseball's greatest player, if not the game's fiercest competitor. He was a vicious individual throughout his life, and apparently became more and more reclusive with advancing age.

Ty Cobb was a lot of things to a lot of people. He obviously accomplished much as a major league baseball player, setting record after record and becoming baseball's first millionaire through his high salary (for the day) and calculated investments. One of those investments was the purchase of stock in a little-known Atlanta beverage company called Coca-Cola.

"The Georgia Peach" from all accounts was not a well-liked man, on or off the baseball field. But, long after retiring from baseball, Cobb "scored" on two major projects that he took on late in life – the Cobb Memorial Hospital in Royston that he established with a $100,000 donation and the Ty Cobb Educational Foundation that he established for Georgia youngsters who could not afford to go to college.

Ty Cobb is gone from this earth, but both of his special projects are thriving to this day...and getting stronger with the years.

Cobb donated funds for the hospital in his hometown back in 1945 "in loving memory of my mother and father" and flew across the country in January 1950 for its formal opening. "I don't believe there'll be any time in my life when I'll be happier than I am today," Cobb said in <u>My Life in Baseball: The True Record</u>, his autobiography co-authored with Al Stump. *(See architectural drawing of hospital on page vi)*

"There isn't much I can say," Cobb continued, from the platform before three thousand old friends. "I wish I had the gift [of speech]. But I want you to know that this building and all that is in it belongs to you people, here where I used to live. It is for you friends for whom I've always had it in my heart."

In his book, Cobb said the modern hospital in rural Georgia was built by funds that "came my way because I was a baseball player."

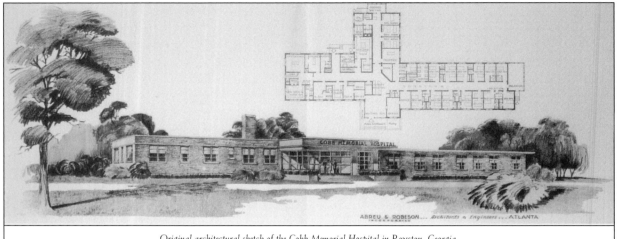

Original architectural sketch of the Cobb Memorial Hospital in Royston, Georgia.

Asking himself if the hospital would be standing years later if he had defied God, Cobb answered "I know that it would not."

"Neither would there be a Cobb Educational Foundation, which finances high-caliber boys and girls through college in such important fields as medicine, engineering, social sciences, art, and research of many kinds," he wrote. "By the several hundred, the Foundation can point to students and graduates whose future deeds for man's good will be immeasurable."

At the time he was writing his autobiography, Cobb was nearing the end of his life. The Foundation had been announced in late 1953, and the first scholarships were awarded in July 1954. "For a long time, I have been interested in doing something along educational lines," Cobb was quoted in the November 30, 1953, news release that announced the Ty Cobb Educational Foundation. "I missed something in life...I can get awfully sentimental about something like this. I can cry too. It runs in my family."

Originally named for Cobb's father, the Ty Cobb Educational Fund was a great undertaking for the former baseball great. His intent was to help only those who showed a determination to succeed. "We want stars – stars in medicine, in law, in teaching, in engineering and in life," Cobb told *The Saturday Evening Post*. "We want the Lincolnesque characters from the mountains and the fields."

"We want to be identified with their success," he said in <u>Cobb: A Biography</u>, written by Al Stump.

"I feed on the warm feeling that I have inside me," he added.

Cobb often tired of talking about baseball when people came to talk with him during his late years, according to Charles C. Alexander in his book, <u>Ty Cobb</u>. "But when the subject of his scholarship fund came up, he would become animated and his eyes would glitter as they had when he taught hitting."

The work of the students had been "phenomenal," he told a visitor in 1958. And, although he had personally met only about ten of the scholarship recipients, he knew they were all the kind of people he originally had in mind. Pulling out dossiers on each of them, he talked glowingly about their progress and admitted a preference for north Georgia youth. "I mean their faces," he said, showing pictures of each. "They've got character."

Later in this report you will read about the many times that Ty Cobb praised "his" students. Before their deaths, Foundation board members, Dr. Merritt E. Hoag and Dr. S. Walter Martin, talked about meeting with Cobb during the late years of his life and the many tears he shed while reading application letters from students. Dr. Hoag served on the Foundation Board along with Cobb from 1959 until Ty's death in 1961. Dr. Martin didn't officially join the board until 1963, but as a Vice Chancellor under then University System Chancellor and Cobb Foundation Chairman Harmon W. Caldwell, he also met with Cobb during the late 1950s and early 1960s.

When the Ty Cobb Educational Foundation celebrated its 50th anniversary in 2003, it was reported that almost $10 million had been provided for more than 6,800 residents of Georgia and that perhaps no one would have guessed that could be accomplished in

50 years...no one, that is, except Ty Cobb. It all started with 250 shares of Coca-Cola stock in 1953, and on the following pages of this 50th anniversary publication you will discover just how much has been accomplished. The news release follows:

July, 2003
FOR IMMEDIATE RELEASE
(Ty Cobb Educational Foundation's 50th Anniversary)

Fifty years ago, nobody would have guessed that Tyrus R Cobb, one of the greatest major league baseball players of his day, could dream up and establish an educational foundation that would provide almost $10 million for more than 6,800 Georgia residents to attend college...no one, that is, except Ty Cobb himself.

A baseball immortal, "The Georgia Peach" announced the establishment of the Cobb Educational Fund at an Atlanta news conference in late 1953, depositing 250 shares of Coca-Cola stock with Trust Company of Georgia, the Fund's permanent Trustee. Cobb named a four-person scholarship board, consisting originally of Dr. Daniel C. Elkin, M.D., professor of surgery at Emory University Hospital; Dr. Harmon W. Caldwell, Chancellor of the University System of Georgia; Dr. Fred W. Rankin of Lexington, Ky.; and Mrs. Tyrus R. Cobb.

Ty Cobb in 1947 aboard a ship in California.

Recipients of Cobb scholarships would have to make it through their freshman years on their own — a requirement that still stands 50 years later — before qualifying for a grant. Cobb's intent was to help needy Georgians who had shown a determination to succeed.

After a slow start, the Cobb Foundation has grown into a major contributor for Georgia students attending colleges and universities across the country. The scholarship program was established in 1953, and six awards totaling $2,800 were made during the 1954-55 academic year. Ten years later, the number of scholarships was at 72 with over $29,000 being awarded.

At their 50th anniversary meeting in July, 2003, the current scholarship board awarded $528,000 to a total of 221 students. The record amount awarded during

any given year was the $648,334 for the 2001-02 academic year, and more than a half million dollars have been provided for Georgia residents during each of the last seven years.

After the first year in 1953, Ty Cobb himself joined the scholarship board along with the Hon. Albert B. "Happy" Chandler, former Governor (1935-39) and U.S. Senator (1939-45) from Kentucky, and later Commissioner of Baseball (1945-51). Chandler replaced Dr. Rankin while another famous baseball player, Hall of Famer Earle Combs of Richmond, Ky., replaced Mrs. Cobb on the board. Combs had led off the famous "Murderer's Row" batting order for the Yankees that featured Babe Ruth and Lou Gehrig.

When Dr. Elkin passed away in 1958, Dr. Caldwell began his chairmanship role from his Atlanta office. Dr. Caldwell was named Chairman Emeritus in 1977 and Dr. H. Prentice "Dean" Miller of Emory University succeeded him as chairman. Dr. Harry S. Downs, president of Clayton Junior College (now Clayton College & State University), joined the board in 1977 and was appointed chairman in 1982, a position he currently holds.

Former members of the board include: Dr. Elkin (1953-58); Dr. Caldwell (1953-77); Dr. Rankin (1953-54); Mrs. Cobb (1953-54); Chandler (1954-60); Combs (1954-61); Dr. Charles S. Kennedy of Detroit (1954-63); Dr. Miller (1959-85); Dr. Merritt E. Hoag, President, North Georgia College (1959-94); Dr. S. Walter Martin, Vice Chancellor of the Board of Regents and later President at Valdosta State College (1963-2000); and Dr. Derrell C. Roberts, President, Dalton Junior College (1984-2002).

Current members include Dr. Downs, now retired as president of Clayton College & State University (1977-present); Dr. Walter Y. Murphy, retired president of LaGrange College (1987-present); and Dr. Francis J. Tedesco, M.D., retired president of The Medical College of Georgia (1998-present).

Cobb was "probably the most volatile, fear-inspiring presence in baseball history and was unparalleled as a performer for most of his 24-year career in the major leagues," according to author Charles C. Alexander in his book, Ty Cobb. "Proud, hypersensitive and highly intelligent, he was determined to be the greatest ballplayer of his day, and he fiercely battled anyone who stood in his path."

Cobb's brilliant career, spent mostly with the Detroit Tigers, included a lifetime batting average of .366. He broke in with the Tigers in 1905, playing in 41 games and batting only .240. It would be his only year to hit below .300 — and he broke the .400 mark in 1911, playing in 146 games and batting .420. Cobb "dropped" to .409 in 140 games the next year. He set dozens of records before leaving the game in 1928.

When the Hall of Fame for baseball's greatest players was established in the mid 1930s, the 226 members of the Baseball Writers Association of America were polled to select the first group of immortals. When the votes were counted in early 1936, Cobb had received 222 votes, only four shy of unanimity. Babe Ruth, who had retired the year before, and Honus Wagner were tied for second with 215.

When Ty Cobb died in 1961, this native of the little town of Royston, located in Franklin County in northeast Georgia, held 43 different records for batting, base-stealing and durability during his 28-year major league career.

Most of his records have fallen through the years, but his Ty Cobb Educational Foundation, currently celebrating its 50th anniversary, continues to provide funds for Georgia residents to obtain a quality education. The Georgia Peach probably never dreamed it would reach the $10 million level, but it will when awards are announced next year.

Following awards for the coming year, 6,876 Georgians have received scholarships totaling $9,743,123...not to bad for a $150,000 start!

As George Maines said in the opening quote of this Introduction, "they broke into tears and Cobb cried along with them." A longtime friend, Maines also said that he felt the students Cobb supported "filled a void in his life" following the untimely deaths of two of his three sons.

In a 1964 report from Major League Baseball, "Living Memorials Keep Ty Cobb's Fame Alive," Ty Cobb was highly praised. (*see following*)

LIVING MEMORIALS KEEP TY COBB'S FAME ALIVE

There is a Ty Cobb plaque in Baseball's Hall of Fame at Cooperstown, N. Y. There is a larger Ty Cobb plaque at Ponce de Leon Park in Atlanta, Ga. On the outside wall of Tiger Stadium in Detroit is a magnificently-sculptured 4-foot plaque commemorating Detroit's greatest baseball player. In Royston, Ga. (pop. 2,000) the citizens are raising half a million dollars for an ornate Ty Cobb Baseball Shrine, to honor the Royston boy who became the most exciting baseball player of all time.

But Ty Cobb's true memorial lives in the hearts of people; the men and women and children who find surcease from pain in the Cobb Memorial Hospital he built in Royston; the boys and girls who get a college education they could not otherwise afford because of a scholarship provided by the Cobb Educational Foundation.

Cobb was a complex, high-strung man, whose frequent temperamental clashes with individuals, friend and foe alike, tended to obscure the deep underlying love for his fellow men, which he evidenced in many ways throughout his life. In memory of his father, the well-loved superintendent of schools in Royston, Cobb sparked the establishment of the town's hospital in 1950. In 1953, he established the Cobb Scholarship Foundation in Atlanta, Ga. It is an interesting commentary on Cobb's respect for excellence and his insistence that men use their talents and be willing to help themselves that he made his Foundation scholarships available to boys and girls who have completed their freshman year in college and demonstrated exceptional ability, but who need help to stay in college . . . also to boys and girls seeking advanced degrees.

The baseball feats of Tyrus Raymond Cobb will live as long as Americans love courage, daring and the fire of a great competitor. The human kindness of this graduate of major league baseball will not be forgotten while pain-racked bodies find help from the Cobb Memorial Hospital, and while young minds are given a chance to grow and help the world through the Cobb Foundation.

Ty Cobb was a widely known individual both in baseball and in other circles. Of course, there were many in baseball that both loved and hated him.

Throughout his career, he had been General Douglas MacArthur's favorite ball player. "MacArthur, indeed, gushed about Cobb," Stump said in Cobb: A Biography. In January 1960, MacArthur invited Cobb to visit him at his retirement home in the Waldorf Towers in New York City. But after a short visit, Cobb said he was not feeling well and prepared to leave. "We probably won't see each other again, Ty," the aged MacArthur said emotionally.

Cobb knew other big names of his day. While putting the final touches to Cobb's book, My Life in Baseball: The True Record, Cobb and Stump uncovered letters to him from Presidents Theodore Roosevelt, Woodrow Wilson, and Warren Harding. He also knew President William Howard Taft, and maybe others.

In addition, there were letters from such fans as Mark Twain, Thomas A. Edison, Will Rogers, Connie Mack, Damon Runyon, Douglas Fairbanks, William Randolph Hearst, Ernest Hemingway, Bobby Jones, Knute Rockne, and many others. He was a personal friend of writer Grantland Rice of the Atlanta newspapers, and also of Taylor Spinks of the *Sporting News*.

As mentioned earlier, Cobb collaborated on an autobiography with the sportswriter Al Stump. The writer relied heavily on Cobb's memory, failing to check the accuracy of Cobb's recall. The book <u>My Life in Baseball: The True Record</u> was published just months after Cobb's death. Although filled with factual errors and half-truths, it is considered one of the greatest sports autobiographies.

In 1994 Stump wrote his own book, entitled <u>Cobb: A Biography</u>. This time, Stump was more meticulous in his research and filled in some of the details missing from the autobiography. Cobb's work with Stump was the basis for the 1994 movie *Cobb*, starring Tommy Lee Jones and directed by Ron Shelton.

When Ty Cobb died on July 17, 1961, the New York *Herald Tribune* ran the following editorial the next morning:

The redoubtable Tyrus Raymond Cobb, sharp of mind and spike, is dead. It would take a long parade of superlatives to re-enact his career, for his were talents of unmatched variety.

Ted Williams could hit, but his running left room for jeers. Pepper Martin could run, but he was no Babe Ruth at the plate. Babe Ruth became the undisputed Sultan of Swat, but nobody wanted him around as a manager. And many is the athlete who lives the well-rounded baseball life but whose efforts to earn an honest living off the diamond end in the poorhouse.

Ty Cobb shone with multilateral brilliance. In baseball (he once held ninety records), and in business afterward (he became a multi-millionaire) he scored consistently. After retiring from the game in 1928 his name lived on as a symbol of championship performance. A gentleman that never came within earshot of his crackling bat argued his prowess and publicized his feats.

It is not for us to say that his aggressive pre-emption of the base paths was or was not in keeping with the book. We'll leave that to the untiring tongues of grandstand umpires.

Of Ty Cobb, let it be said simply that he was the world's greatest ballplayer.

TY COBB AT TURNER FIELD — *Ty Cobb died before major league baseball came to Georgia, but the Georgia native still has a place at Atlanta's Turner Field. Sculptor Felix de Weldon provided this "Ty slide" in 1977, and it has a prominent place along with other Braves stars in front of Turner Field.*

CHAPTER ONE

The Cobb Family

The honorable and honest Cobb blood...never will be subjected. It bows to no wrong nor to any man...the Cobbs have their ideals and God help anyone who strives to bend a Cobb away from such.

– Ty Cobb, 1927, in a letter to U.S. Congressman Robert H. Clancy - taken from Cobb: A Biography by Al Stump.

WILLIAM HERSCHEL COBB
The Father

William Herschel Cobb was a successful school teacher, principal, newspaper publisher, mayor, county commissioner, and state senator. Originally from Murphy, North Carolina, he was a graduate of North Georgia Agricultural College in Dahlonega and became the principal and only full-time teacher at The Narrows, a small community located in extreme northern Banks County, Georgia. He later moved to Royston to teach and became a well-known citizen of this small town located in the southeastern corner of Franklin County.

W. H. Cobb died in the early morning hours of August 9, 1905, when he apparently was attempting to sneak back into his Royston home. His wife, Amanda, could not see who was at her bedroom window and shot him with a shotgun. A major shaping force in Ty Cobb's youth, the younger Cobb had adored his father, and very much wanted to please him. This untimely death, while Ty Cobb was away playing minor league baseball, was a blow the younger Cobb possibly never overcame.

"My father had his head blown off with a shotgun when I was 18 years old – *by a member of my own family,*" Cobb related late in his life. "I didn't get over that. I've never gotten over it." It was possibly the first time in his life that Cobb had been able to say that much about how W. H. Cobb had died. Even then, he couldn't name his mother as the one who had pulled the trigger.

AMANDA CHITWOOD COBB
The Mother

When, at age 20, W. H. Cobb moved to The Narrows, he fell in love with the daughter of Caleb Chitwood, the most prosperous person in the community. Amanda Chitwood, only 12 years old, married W. H. Cobb during the summer of 1883. However, the marriage was not consummated for a year – possibly longer – so the new couple was slow in starting a family, unusual in those days. Ty Cobb, their first child, was born on December 18, 1886, when Amanda was 15. John Paul followed in 1888 and four years later, a daughter, Florence Leslie.

Amanda Cobb was charged with voluntary manslaughter following the fatal shooting of her husband in 1905 but was found not guilty by a jury trial that had been delayed until late spring 1906.

Amanda Cobb died at age 65 in October 1936 and was buried near her husband in the cemetery in Royston.

TYRUS RAYMOND COBB
The First Child of William Herschel and Amanda Chitwood Cobb *(See information beginning on Page 5)*

JOHN PAUL COBB
The Brother

Paul Cobb, Ty Cobb's younger brother, played baseball briefly at Georgia Tech and later became a fairly good hitter in semipro ball, climbing high enough to be drafted by the St. Louis Browns in 1908. But, being the younger brother of Ty Cobb apparently was too much to overcome for he bounced around the minors until quitting baseball in 1916 to re-enroll at Georgia Tech. After serving in the army during the First World War, he eventually went into the real estate business in Florida.

FLORENCE LESLIE COBB
The Sister

Florence Cobb lived with her mother until Amanda Cobb's death in 1936. Crippled for a long time because of arthritis, she was unable to look after herself. She ended up living most of her remaining years at her brother Paul's home in Sarasota, Florida, until her death in 1944 at age 51. However, she spent one brief period of time living with Ty Cobb in California.

CHARLOTTE "CHARLIE" MARION LOMBARD COBB
First Wife of Tyrus Raymond Cobb

Charlie Lombard, barely 17, became the bride of Ty Cobb, age 21, in Augusta on August 6, 1908. The daughter of Roswell Lombard, a prominent Augustan, Charlie and her baseball-playing husband later spent the off season at the Lombard estate south of town. Charlie and Ty Cobb had five children – Ty Jr. (born in January 1910), Shirley Marion (June 1911), Roswell

Cobb's father, William Herschel Cobb.

Herschel (October 1916), Beverly (Fall of 1920), and James Howell "Jimmy" (July 1921).

Charlie Cobb filed for divorce in early 1931 after Ty had left Augusta to find a new home in California. She later withdrew the proceedings and moved to Atherton, California, with Ty and their children in 1932. Charlie filed and withdrew divorce papers two additional times and continued to live with Ty until 1939 when she left Atherton and moved into a place of her own in Menlo Park, California. Their two daughters, who had not yet married, divided their time between their separated parents.

Then, in March of 1947, Charlie filed her fourth and last divorce action in Redwood City, California. Later, their lawyers determined it would be easier to agree on a property settlement if they were to withdraw the suit in California and move it to Reno, Nevada, where Cobb had bought a home a few years earlier. The divorce became final in late 1947, although terms of the settlement never became public record.

Although Ty Cobb took another wife two years later, Charlie Cobb apparently never lost touch with her longtime husband. When Cobb died in 1961, she came to Atlanta from her home in Menlo Park along with her three children who were still living – Jimmy, Shirley and Beverly (Herschel died in 1951 and Ty Jr. died in 1952). The family was at the hospital when Cobb passed away on July 17, 1961. *(See August 7, 1961, letter to Mrs. Charlie Lombard Cobb from H. Prentice Miller on pages 8-10.)*

TYRUS RAYMOND COBB, JR.
The First Child of Ty and Charlie

An established major leaguer, heading into his sixth season with Detroit, Ty was ready to begin his family with Charlie. Tyrus Raymond Cobb, Jr., was born on January 30, 1910, at The Oaks, the Lombard estate south of Augusta. "New right fielder," Ty wired the Detroit sports editors, telling of his nine-pound boy.

But, all did not turn out as planned for the newest

Cobb. Raised by his mother and private school teachers (since his dad was always gone) Ty Jr. was involved in one scrape after another while enrolled at Richmond Academy in Augusta and later at Princeton University. When he flunked out of Princeton, he entered Yale University and became captain of Yale's tennis team. In 1930, he ran into more trouble with the law and was eventually bailed out by his father, who then informed the 21-year-old that there would be no further communication between them. A major disappointment to his father, Ty Jr. had become Cobb's main problem as a parent.

By the late 1930s, Ty Jr. had finally settled down. Deciding on a career in medicine, he gained admission to the Medical College of South Carolina in Charleston. In 1942, he finished his M.D. with a specialty in gynecology and obstetrics, married Mary Frances Dunn of Daytona Beach, Florida, and set up practice in Dublin, Georgia.

He continued to practice there, living with his wife and three children, until an inoperable brain tumor was discovered in 1951. Ty Jr. died at his mother's home in Menlo Park, California, where, hopelessly ill, he had relocated for care. He was only 42 years old at the time of his death.

Not long before he died – almost 20 years after the Yale University falling out – Ty Jr., the boy who favored tennis over baseball, was finally reconciled with his famous father. Late in Ty Cobb's life, the baseball great visited his son's wife, Mary, and three children in Florida and got to know them for the first time.

SHIRLEY MARION COBB (BECKWITH)
The Second Child

The Cobbs' second child, a daughter named Shirley Marion, was born in Detroit in late June 1911. Cobb, in the midst of the best batting season of his career, was talking about making 300 hits in a season and breaking the all-time high batting average of .492. He fell a little short, with 248 hits and a .420 batting average, but now he was an established star in the majors with a son and a daughter to provide for.

In 1928, when Cobb was in his final year with the Athletics (and final year in the majors), Philadelphia scheduled a spring training game in Augusta on March 16. Shirley Cobb, then 16, begged her father to pass up the game and come watch her perform in a horse show. Cobb ignored the plea and suited up for the game.

BIRD DOG LOVERS – Cobb, son Herschel, and golf champion Bobby Jones discuss this Irish Setter at Field Dog Trials in Waynesboro, Georgia. During the off season and into retirement years, Cobb was an avid golfer, hunter, and breeder of bird dogs.

After the move to California, Shirley married and operated a bookstore in Palo Alto. She died at age 80 in 1991, 30 years after making the 1961 trip to Atlanta to see her ailing father for the last time before eventually attending his funeral. (*See August 7, 1961, letter on pages 8-10.*)

ROSWELL HERSCHEL COBB
The Third Child

The third of the Cobbs' five children, named for Cobb's father, was Roswell Herschel, born in Augusta in October 1916. Ty didn't make it from St. Louis to Augusta in time for the birth and didn't stay around too long afterwards, for he had to take care of World Series duties – not as a player, but as a reporter.

To his father's great pleasure, Herschel was a good schoolboy athlete. But, his life on earth was a short one. In April 1951 he suffered a sudden heart attack at the age of 34, leaving a wife and three children. His shocking death came just over a year before Ty Jr. passed away, making this a dark period in the life of Ty Cobb.

BEVERLY COBB (MCLAREN)
The Fourth Child

The Cobb's second daughter, Beverly, was born in Detroit near the end of the 1919 baseball season. Charlie Cobb was slow in recovering from her fourth childbirth, so Ty stayed close to Augusta during the off season.

Although not at home much during the younger years of the children, Cobb was very concerned about them when he was around. He worried, for example, that Beverly would somehow be injured in the archery classes she took at an early age.

As a 19-year-old, she and her younger brother Jimmy traveled with their father to the 1939 opening of the National Baseball Museum and Hall of Fame in Cooperstown, NY. But later in life, while married and a well-to-do resident of California, Beverly found it harder and harder to put up with her father's contemptuous attitude toward their mother.

Still, like her mother, older sister, and brother, she returned to Georgia for Ty's death and funeral. (*See August 7, 1961, letter on pages 8-10.*)

JAMES HOWELL "JIMMY" COBB
The Fifth Child

The final child born to Charlie and Ty Cobb was the hardest delivery for Charlie. Born prematurely in Detroit on July 23, 1921, Jimmy Cobb left his mother with severe postpartum complications. She returned to Georgia to recuperate from her fifth childbirth, and both she and her newest baby remained sick for a long time.

Later in life, Jimmy Cobb described his father as a strict disciplinarian who was sparing in his praise, especially of his three sons. But he also remembered his father tucking him in at night and playing catch with him in the back yard, as well as worrying about him getting hurt while playing grade-school football.

Following the family's move to California, Jimmy graduated from New Mexico Military Institute and entered the Army during World War II in 1942. Ty Cobb was at dockside in San Francisco to greet his youngest son upon his return from the Pacific region early in 1946; Jimmy couldn't hang around – he had to hurry off to Idaho to join his wife and baby in Twin Falls. His brother, Herschel, was waiting to make him a partner in the local Coca-Cola bottling plant there.

Near the end of Ty Cobb's life, Jimmy became a successful businessman in Santa Maria, California. And, along with his mother and two sisters, Jimmy was present at Emory Hospital when Ty Cobb passed away on July 17, 1961. (*See August 7, 1961, letter on pages 8-10.*)

FRANCES FAIRBURN COBB
The Second Wife of Ty Cobb

Partially because of the high cost of divorcing Charlie in 1947, Ty Cobb had not planned to marry again. But, two years later, Frances Fairburn, an attractive divorcee and the daughter of a Buffalo, New York, physician whom Cobb had known for several years, caught his eye. The 62-year-old Cobb married the 40-year-old Frances on September 24, 1949, telling newsmen after the wedding that she was "a rare woman who liked to golf, hunt, travel and cook."

When Cobb developed plans for the Ty Cobb Educational Foundation, one of the first four Trustees in 1953 was Frances Cobb. But it was a short arrangement. Frances filed for divorce in September 1955 and resigned from the board late that year. The divorce from her fourth husband was finalized in May 1956.

But, like Cobb's first wife, Frances didn't walk completely away. When Cobb became ill in the fall of 1959, Frances (who had taken back her previous last name of Cass) heard about it and traveled to Cobb's lodge near Lake Tahoe, Nevada. Still carrying plenty of hurts and resentments from their marriage, she offered to stay and care for him. Cobb protested, since they were no longer married, but she stayed for two weeks and eventually convinced him to enter the Scripps Clinic at La Jolla, California, for a thorough physical examination. Once there, the doctors reported that Cobb had diabetes, a weak heart, high blood pressure, an enlarged prostate gland, and other conditions. Later, it was determined he had cancer.

~ REMEMBERING ~
Tyrus Raymond Cobb
December 18, 1886 – July 17, 1961

The eldest of three children, Tyrus Raymond Cobb was born in The Narrows, a scattered group of farms in a valley in extreme northern Banks County, Georgia. Situated in the upper Georgia piedmont just at the edge of the southernmost extension of the Great Smoky Mountains, The Narrows was a geographical expression, appearing on no maps and no post office. The closest town was Cornelia, some three or four miles away in Habersham County.

Ty Cobb's father, a rural school teacher and principal, moved his family frequently during the early years of his life before finally settling in Royston, located in the southeastern corner of Franklin County. His father, Professor W. H. Cobb, eventually became one of Royston's most respected citizens.

In his book, My Life in Baseball: The True Record, one of Cobb's first clear-cut memories was riding on the back of a buggy, bumping along a red clay Georgia road between Commerce and Carnesville where his schoolmaster father was heading to another job. Barefoot and with his legs dangling over the tailgate, Ty was busy winding yarn around a small core ball, trying to complete the task of making a baseball before they reached the next town. "At 11 and 12, I liked to play cow-pasture baseball," he recalled in the book.

"Move ahead just six years, and I have another clear memory," he said, "of sitting alongside manager Bill Armour on the Detroit Tigers' bench, realizing that in a few minutes I'd play my first major league game."

"That Tyrus Cobb had jumped from the buggy tailgate (at the age of 12) all the way into Bennett Park, Detroit, Michigan (at age 18), seemed to me the number one miracle of creation," he concluded.

COBB FAMILY – Shortly after Ty Cobb retired from baseball, he took his family on an around-the-world trip. Pictured on their arrival at Honolulu, en route home from Japan, are (left to right) Charlie, Beverly, Ty, Jimmy, and Herschel.

The life of Ty Cobb is well documented in numerous books and publications, so we won't go into full detail here. Much of his baseball career will be documented in another chapter of this publication, but you can't leave this area without going to a few important events in his life.

For example:

– Ty Cobb's father urged him to study, and perhaps become a lawyer or physician. When Ty went off to play professional baseball, his father sternly warned him, "Don't come home a failure."

– Ty Cobb began his minor league baseball career on April 26, 1904, playing for Augusta. Released after two games, he then proved his abilities at Anniston, AL, and was invited back to play for Augusta. He played the next season for Augusta and on August 9, 1905, received a telegram from Royston that his father had been killed...his mother, they told him, had shot his father.

– Eight days after his father's funeral, with his life turned upside down, Ty Cobb was called up by the Detroit Tigers. On August 30, 1905, at the age of 18, Cobb's 24-year major league baseball career began. (*see Chapter 6, page 123*)

– For nearly a quarter of a century, Ty Cobb made his home in Augusta where, in 1908, he married Charlotte "Charlie" Marion Lombard, the daughter of prominent Augustan Roswell Lombard. Visitors to the Cobb home included golfer Bobby Jones (with whom he also played golf), football coach Knute Rockne, John Philip Sousa, and Atlanta sportswriter Grantland Rice.

– He associated with financiers and industrialists, golfed with President William Howard Taft, and visited President Woodrow Wilson at the White House.

– Cobb invested his money in real estate and securities, and owned an auto dealership in Augusta. His best investments were with Atlanta-based Coca-Cola Company and Detroit-based General Motors.

– Cobb's hobbies included shooting game, playing golf at Augusta Country Club, and later in California, raising bird dogs, and investing his money.

– Ty and Charlie Cobb raised five children and were divorced in 1947; she had filed and withdrawn actions three times before making it final. Ty Cobb married Frances Fairburn two years later, a marriage that lasted until 1956.

– Although Cobb thought he would live his life in Georgia, he moved his family to northern California in 1932. Cobb had fallen in love with the town of Atherton, located about 22 miles south of the San Francisco city limits and three miles or so from Menlo Park (which would be the Cobbs' mailing address).

– From his California home, Cobb played golf most of the year at the many courses built in the Bay Area; hunted wildlife all over the state; hunted big game in Idaho, Wyoming and Canada; fished in mountain streams; and even tried his hand at polo.

– In 1945, as a memorial to his parents, Cobb had decided to build a hospital in his hometown of Royston. He donated $100,000 for the hospital and in January 1950 flew across the country to be on hand for the dedication of Cobb Memorial Hospital.

– A much bigger cause for Cobb in the 1950's was the Cobb Educational Fund, which he announced at a press conference in Atlanta in 1953. (*See page 33.*)

– Late in his life (1957), Cobb was quoted as being "just a lonesome old man" and decided to move back to Georgia from his homes in California and Nevada. He found a spot on Chenoocetah Mountain, located just north of Cornelia and only 22 miles from Royston. He

Cobb (right) with Bob Jones of Georgia, fresh from scoring his "Grand Slam" of golf when the two posed for this shot at Highlands, North Carolina, in late 1930.

made plans to live on the mountain and "be by myself while I rest." But, the house was never built and Cobb ventured back to the West Coast.

– "Ty Cobb always was a taciturn man; he grew more and more reclusive with advancing age, and upon reaching 73 in 1960 he was holed up in a pair of dreary homes worth $5 million in Atherton, California, and at Lake Tahoe, Nevada," Al Stump wrote in his book, Cobb: A Biography. "Baseball's greatest, most thoroughly disliked player of this century lived without electric lights (candles only in one of his hideouts) and without telephone service (in both). The multimillionaire had been estranged from his five children decades earlier. Two wives had charged extreme cruelty in divorces, each deposing that "The Georgia Peach" was uncontrollable when crossed or drunk, or whenever he was reminded of how he had regularly bloodied opponents with his spikes."

– By the fall of 1959, Cobb had been diagnosed with cancer, diabetes, high blood pressure, an enlarged prostate, and Bright's disease, a degenerative kidney disorder. He returned to his Lake Tahoe lodge with painkillers and bourbon to try to ease his constant pain. Continuing his lifelong style of not trusting anyone, Cobb didn't trust the initial diagnosis. So, he went to Georgia to seek advice from doctors he knew, and they found his prostate to be cancerous. He underwent surgery at Emory Hospital, but it did little to help. From this point until the end of his life, the restless Cobb criss-crossed the country, traveling from Nevada to the hospital in Georgia.

– On April 27, 1961 – less than three months prior to his death – Cobb somehow gathered enough strength to make it to Wrigley Field in Los Angeles for

A portrait of the enigmatic Cobb that resides in the museum in his hometown of Royston, Georgia.

the home opener of the new expansion team, the Los Angeles Angels (later, the Anaheim Angels). The ailing Cobb threw out the first ball to keep a promise to Fred Haney, general manager of the Angels, stayed through two innings, and left with the help of his cane and a park attendant. He had seen his last baseball game.

– He checked into Emory Hospital for the last time in June 1961 reportedly bringing with him a paper bag containing a million or so dollars in securities and his Luger pistol. His first wife, Charlie, and other family members came from California to be with him for his final days.

– Tyrus Raymond Cobb died at the age of 74 at Emory University Hospital in Atlanta on July 17, 1961. In his will, Cobb left a quarter of his estate to the Cobb Educational Fund, and the rest of his reputed $11 million he distributed among his children and grandchildren.

– His funeral was perhaps the saddest event associated with Cobb. From all of baseball, the sport that he had dominated for over 20 years, baseball's only representatives were three old players, Ray Schalk, Mickey Cochrane, Nap Rucker, along with Sid Keener from the Hall of Fame. Also there were his first wife, Charlie; his two daughters, Shirley and Beverly; his surviving son, Jimmy; his two sons-in-law; his daughter-in-law, Mary Dunn Cobb (widow of Ty Jr.), and her three children. It is often mentioned that only three major league players showed up at Ty's funeral because he was not liked at all. The real truth is that most of Cobbs' friends in baseball had already passed away. In fact, at the time of Ty's death, Cochrane, his good friend, was already ill with a respiratory ailment and would die some 11 months after Cobb, in June of 1962.

August 7, 1961

Mrs. Charlie Lombard Cobb
Woodside, California

My dear Mrs. Cobb:

From time to time I am going to write you. I am assuming that
James and Mrs. McLaren and Mrs. Beckworth pay you frequent
visits. Although my letters will be addressed to you, I hope that
they will be of interest to your three children.

Let me assure you that you and your three children won my unqualified respect and admiration from the start. I can imagine
no more difficult situation than all of you faced during your
weeks here, and every observation which I made offered the proof
that all of you were truly heroic.

Whenever any or all of you may have occasion to return to Atlanta,
I would deem it an honor and a privilege to have an opportunity to
see you again.

After the funeral I telephoned once to the motel, and on another
occasion I made a trip to your motel. I missed all of you on
both occasions. I simply wanted to pay my respects again and to
be of service if needed.

Many honors have come my way from time to time, but I want you to
know that being invited to serve at Ty's funeral is one of the
very highest and greatest. I shall always cherish being invited
and serving.

The funeral service was impressive and fitting in every fashion.
I know that you will always share with me a feeling that everything about it was completely appropriate.

I know that you met many people at the end of the service,
enough to be hopelessly confusing. Chancellor Harmon W. Caldwell
and Miss McMahon, his secretary, were at Cornelia and Royston

Mrs. Charlie Lombard Cobb (Continued)   August 7, 1961

with me. President Merritt Hoag of North Georgia College at
Dahlonega joined us in Cornelia.

We notified Dr. Kennedy, and after some hesitation and effort he
called and stated that he could not be present. Frankly, I was
much concerned over Dr. Kennedy's health and somewhat feared a
return trip if he attempted to make one. He had seen Ty on
Thursday evening before our meeting of the Trustees on Friday. He
was greatly disturbed over Ty's condition and predicted what
actually happened. He was having an exceedingly difficult time
accepting the idea of the loss of his very close friend.

I read everything in the local press. Some of it pleased me, but
at least some of it caused me anguish. I am afraid that the
American press has little regard for either the person written
about or his family and friends. The fame of a great man extracts
a high price not only of him but also of his family.

It was my privilege to see Ty from time to time during the last two
years. Because my office is close to the Emory Hospital, I could
drop in to see him far more easily than Chancellor Caldwell could
pay him a visit from downtown. I can assure you that helping Georgia
boys and girls gave Ty a great deal of satisfaction. I am sure that
it had a somewhat stabilizing and comforting effect upon him as his
illnesses increased.

Again, I want to pledge to you that whatever income is available
each year, we shall give to deserving Georgia boys and girls. We
have had far more worthy applicants than we could help without our
making any public announcement in advance about the fund. I have
served on many difficult committees in my lifetime. In recent
years we at Emory have had approximately 700 applicants for 72
places in our Medical School. You can well understand what a
terrible and terrifying assignment it is to be a part of those who

Mrs. Charlie Lombard Cobb (Continued)   August 7, 1961

make the choices.

But I can assure you that our meeting of the Cobb Educational Foundation Trustees on July 14th was equally difficult. Twenty-five students whom the Foundation had helped in earlier years were still in school, were doing well, and merited continued support. We had ninety-eight new applicants and agreed that we would reduce the ninety-eight to fifteen and therefore have a total of forty for the coming year. Each member of the Committee had examined the applications earlier, but we spent the entire day on them. We finally chose the twenty-one as having the greatest need and possibilities, and we simply could not or did not have the heart to reduce the number to fifteen. Chancellor Caldwell said that there was some scholarship money available to the various branches of the University System and he felt that some of those whom we had chosen might receive such a scholarship. On that basis we kept the twenty-one.

Vice President Alfred Boylston of the Trust Department of the Trust Company of Georgia is a personal friend of mine. He tells me that within a matter of a month or two some preliminary report can be made about the future status of the Cobb Educational Foundation. In behalf of all of us who are trustees, we want to assure you that every dollar which comes to the Foundation will be spent to help Georgia boys and girls in as wise a fashion as our full efforts permit. It is indeed an honor to each of us to so serve Ty and many Georgia boys and girls.

It was indeed a privilege to meet you and your family. I shall never know how each of you stood up so well under exceedingly difficult conditions. I hope that by this time you have at least somewhat recovered from what I know was an almost impossibly agonizing trip to Georgia.

Sincerely yours,

H. Prentice Miller
Trustee
Cobb Educational Foundation

HPM:wg

P. S. I shall be happy to hear from you or any other member of your
       family. My address is Emory University, Atlanta 22, Georgia.

CHAPTER TWO

Getting Started

For a long time, I have been interested in doing something along educational lines."

– Tyrus R. Cobb in a November 30, 1953, release announcing his new Cobb Educational Foundation

There is little, if any, documentation about when, or why, Ty Cobb decided to start the Cobb Educational Foundation. Undoubtedly, there had been much communication between Ty and Dr. Daniel C. Elkin, professor of medicine and head of the medical department at Emory University, before the start of the Foundation in late 1953. But, since there was no office for the Foundation prior to its beginning, there are no files to indicate this communication.

The earliest letter in the files was dated November 10, 1953. "Dear Doc," it starts. "Yours of 6th Nov. received today."

Obviously, Dr. Elkin had written to Ty Cobb on November 6, but a copy of the letter is not on file. It appears the two had been communicating for some time about what has become one of the best things Ty Cobb managed to dream up in his lifetime.

"I have everything here in readiness and a talk with you and Dr. Caldwell to o.k. everything," Cobb wrote in his November 10 letter to "Doc." Dr. Caldwell, as referred to, was Dr. Harmon W. Caldwell, chancellor of the University System of Georgia. (*See a copy of the 2-page letter on pages 18-19.*)

The subject of the letter was an attempt to set up a meeting to announce the formation of the Cobb Foundation. "Now if between, say [the] 24th and 25th of November, and December 1st will suit you, I will advise exact date," Cobb wrote. "I will be there. I would like to get it completed in 1953."

In the letter from Menlo Park, California, he said that his wife, Frances, had left for Buffalo, New York, and would meet him in Atlanta for the announcement.

Another letter from Cobb, this one a seven-pager and dated November 13, 1953, refers to a November 10 letter from Dr. Elkin, but that letter from "Doc" also is missing from the files. "Yours of 11/10/53 just received and as you see I hasten to reply," Cobb wrote. Then, he launched into a long, and sometimes hard to follow, discussion about "securing some fine old bourbon." (*See a copy of the 7-page letter on pages 20-23.*)

Finally, in the middle of page three of his letter, Cobb wrote, "Enough of this." And, he immediately changed the subject to the upcoming meeting in Atlanta. "I am happy to know you will be available between [the] 24th and Dec. 2nd," he said. "It fits into my plans perfectly."

He added that Frances would have her duties completed in Buffalo, NY and would be able to join him in Atlanta. He also talked about going by St. Louis, Missouri, where a friend would be honored on December 23, and stopping off in Nashville, Tennessee, for a visit at the Nashville Banner on November 24. "So, if you can say for sure any date between [the] 24th and 28th…then you set the date and write me so I can make permanent my plans," Cobb wrote.

Then, he went into a discussion about a Mr. Johnson from Royston whom they had discussed as a potential trustee for the Foundation. It appears that Mr. Johnson had not followed through on a request by Cobb for placement of paintings of him, his mother, and his father at the new Cobb Memorial Hospital in Royston. Cobb had asked a relative to check on the paintings and found that they had been placed in another part of the hospital; he obviously was not pleased.

And, perhaps more importantly, Johnson had not responded with a letter to Cobb on a timely basis.

Dr. Harmon W. Caldwell

"I have changed my mind as to Johnson's being a trustee with yourself and Dr. Caldwell," Cobb said in his November 13 letter. "Now I ask you, do we need or have to have a third member, and if so, please be thinking of a proper person that will serve. I have Johnson's medallion with name finished and complete, but I have been to the jewelers here and they have assured me they can remove Johnson's name and put on another, etc."

The "Johnson" referred to likely was Col. Linton S. Johnson, who was listed as a Trustee for Cobb Memorial Hospital on a letterhead that Cobb used in writing a letter on January 17, 1960. *(See letterhead on page 91.)*

The medallion mentioned apparently was something dear to Cobb's heart. In a news release that followed the announcement ceremony, it reported that "The Georgia Peach" presented handsome gold medal-

lions to both Dr. Elkin and Dr. Caldwell "who will serve, along with either Cobb or his wife, as trustees of the foundation."

More on that later in this chapter, but let's go back to the November 13 letter.

"Doc, please pardon the infliction of such a long letter, also such details, but I have to give you the picture," Cobb said, changing pace on the next-to-last page of his letter.

"In closing, I hope all will go off properly," he added, saying also that it was a good idea to invite the press and news services to be on hand for the short ceremony of presentations and the announcement of the Foundation. "I have revealed my intent to some and they want to be there," he said.

Cobb added that he would like to follow the announcement by spending a day to complete matters with representatives from Trust Company Bank, who would handle the funds, and with Furman Smith, his attorney who was setting up the legal documents for the Foundation. After signing off in his usual manner (I am, Sincerely, Ty), Cobb added a footnote: "written but not re-read, ha!"

Then comes a typewritten letter, author unknown that appears to be a news release. Dated November 30, 1953, the letter reported that the announcement of the Foundation had been made on November 27.

The letter (or release) follows:

Atlanta, Ga.

Ty Cobb, whose record as the game's greatest player has been immortalized in the Hall of Fame, made a lasting contribution to another field in which he is interested, when he announced the establishment of the Cobb Educational Foundation to help qualified students continue their college educations.

In making the announcement here, November 27, The Georgia Peach presented handsome gold medallions to Dr. Dan C. Elkin, professor of medicine and head of the medical department of Emory University, Atlanta, and Dr. Harmon Caldwell, head of all higher educational institutions in Georgia, who will serve, along with either Cobb or his wife, as trustees of the foundation. (See medallion on page 16.)

"For a long time, I have been interested in doing something along educational lines," Cobb said. His father, William H. Cobb, was active in educational matters and, as a Georgia state senator, worked for improved schools and higher pay for teaching personnel. He was the first man in the country to evolve the idea of consolidating rural schools, in 1902, and crusaded for the plan by combining "little red schoolhouses" to provide better educational facilities.

The Cobb Educational Foundation will select deserving applicants, after their freshman year in college, and will aid them financially through the completion of their studies. The trustees will decide on the recipients on the basis of the students' records and after personal interviews. Both boys and girls will be eligible for the assistance and their field of study will not be restricted.

"Naturally, they will be limited in number to fit my purse in donations," Cobb explained. He plans to make yearly contributions to the foundation. In preparing for the project, he said, "for three years, all the fees that I was fortunate enough to receive from magazines, radio, TV, testimonials, etc., have been earmarked for the fund."

Cobb, who now resides in San Francisco, made a special trip to his native state to announce his benefaction.

(See a copy of release on page 24.)

The actual event must have been a day of celebration, especially for Ty and Frances Cobb as well as for doctors Elkin and Caldwell. And, another original "player" in the formation of the Foundation was mentioned in a December 2, 1953, letter. Unsigned, but apparently from Dr. Elkin, the letter was to Ty Cobb, who had returned to his home in Menlo Park, California (located near San Francisco which the news release reported).

"We certainly enjoyed being with you and Frances, and I hope we can renew these visits on many occasions," Dr. Elkin wrote. "I am particularly pleased that things went off to your liking, as they certainly did to mine, regarding the announcement about the foundation. Again, I want to thank you for the beautiful medallion. I am writing Fred all about it and sending him the news clippings."

The "Fred" mentioned in the letter was Dr. Fred Rankin of Lexington, Kentucky, an original member of the board. Dr. Rankin, who served as president of the American College of Surgeons and was past president of the American Medical Association, apparently was a longtime and good friend of Dr. Elkin's.

Although there is no documentation about how Dr. Rankin was added to the board, his name probably came up following Ty's November 13 letter to Dr. Elkin.

In his December 2 letter to Cobb, Dr. Elkin reported that a number of applications for awards had already been received and that he would "attempt shortly to get the idea over to the press that the scholarships are limited to those students who have completed at least their freshman year in college." He said that most of the early applications were from high school students.

"With this correction, and with the help of Dr. Caldwell, we will get up a regular application form, a copy of which I will send you as soon as possible," Dr. Elkin added.

Announcement of the Cobb Foundation attracted national news as the following clipping from TIME, dated December 7, 1953, relates:

"Baseball's famed Georgia Peach, Tyrus Raymond ("Ty") Cobb, 66, whose own education ended with high school, announced that he will set up a fund big enough to help three or four bright, needy Georgia students through colleges and universities each year. The scholarships will be "definitely not athletic." Said Ty: "I missed something in life...I can get awfully sentimental about something like this. I can cry, too. It runs in my family."

And a letter to Dr. Elkin from The New York Times dated December 2 noted that the paper was planning an article on the Cobb Educational Foundation and "would appreciate your help in getting the facts straight." Dr. Elkin's secretary responded to the request from Mr. Joseph Nolan of the Sunday Department of *The New York Times*, noting that Dr. Elkin was out of the city and would respond upon his return.

Elkin's three-page response followed on December 17, 1953. *(See pages 25-27.)*

Several key elements about the Foundation were explained in the letter, including the naming of the original Board of Trustees: Dr. Elkin, Dr. Caldwell, Mrs. Cobb, and Dr. Rankin. Here are additional thoughts:

"The amount of the fund has not been announced, nor will it be, but I can say that it will give partial aid each year to some eight to twenty students, depending upon the available funds and the need of scholarship aid in individual cases.

"Scholarships are open to residents of Georgia who have finished at least the freshman year in an accredited college.

"The scholarship funds are outright gifts and not loans but will only partly cover the students [*sic*] expenses.

"Mr. Cobb will play no active part in the choosing of students although he will certainly take an active inter-est in their careers and will undoubtedly make every effort to know them personally."

On page 2 of the letter, Dr. Elkin tried to answer how Ty Cobb became interested in such an endeavor. "Mr. Cobb has been fortunate in his investments and, as you probably know, is an extremely keen and active man. His own education stopped at the end of high school and he has always felt that he missed something. I have heard him express this on numerous occasions, in not going to college.

"His father was a college graduate, a well educated man. He was superintendent of the schools of Franklin County, Georgia, and as a member of the Georgia State Senate, he was primarily interested in promoting educational facilities, particularly in raising the pay for teachers and in the consolidation of rural schools, in which he took a lead.

"Mr. Cobb is a sentimentalist and has a great feeling for his family. On this account he built a hospital in Royston, Georgia, in memory of his father and mother. This has been in successful operation since 1951.

"I believe it was in 1904, when Mr. Cobb was sev-

One of Cobb's jerseys from the Detroit Tigers that resides in the Cobb Museum.

enteen years old and when he had a local high school record as a baseball player that he made the decision to try out for professional baseball. Meanwhile, his father had entered him at the University of Georgia. At that time, the South Atlantic League was organized and Ty wrote to each of eight clubs asking for a tryout. Only Augusta responded and they told him that he could try out at his own expense. Then came the question of breaking the news to his father, and after an all night session the old man gave in at 3:00 A.M. and Ty made off for Augusta, trying out as a utility infielder.

"It so happened that the first baseman became ill and since there were but few players, the center fielder was moved to first and Ty had a chance in the out field where he played two games, making three hits and stealing two bases. The first baseman then recovered and Ty was released. He played that summer in a semiprofessional league at Anniston, Alabama. During this time, he would slip into drug stores, furniture stores, and other business establishments and use their stationary in writing anonymous letters to Grantland Rice, then with *The Atlanta Journal*, extolling the virtues of this young Cobb. Rice finally took some notice of this avalanche of recommendations and Augusta recalled him and, I believe, he played there about a month when he was bought by Detroit for $500 plus a $200 bonus for reporting late that season. You know the rest of the story.

"I might add that all the money which he has received from newspaper and magazine articles and testimonials has been kept separate for this fund and to it he has also added, and will continue to add, from his private resources."

"*The Atlanta Constitution* of Saturday, November 28th, carried an article by Furman Bisher, sports editor of *The Constitution*, which is informative and fairly accurate, and *The Atlanta Journal-Constitution* of Sunday, November 29th, carried a column by Ralph McGill, editor of the *Atlanta Constitution*. Both of these may be of some help to you in this story.

"I might add that Ty has gone into this matter after considerable thought and consultation and that his wife has been an eager helpmate in his deliberations. He has no delusions about the ability of the trustees to pick outstanding people because he has said to me on numerous occasions, 'If we can pick one winner before

I die, I will think the project worth-while. I have seen too many well advertised boys come to training camp who never made the big leagues and I doubt one in fifty of the yearlings sold at Keenland and Saratoga ever win a stake.'

"At a press conference he was asked if these were athletic scholarships and he replied, 'No.' A reporter then asked him to expand on this and he rather laconically said, 'Absolutely no.'

"Cobb still maintains a keen interest in sports but he reads widely and well and has an exceptional education. He much prefers to talk upon subjects of general interest rather than sports, although at times he can tell wonderful stories of his athletic career. He writes long and interesting letters regarding his trips and regarding his philanthropies, but only to intimate friends who have some interest in his projects, and I might add that in the numerous letters which I have received from him I have never seen a grammatical error and he has no secretary like you and I to pick up his mistakes.

"I hope I have been of some help to you in this story. If I can be of further help, I trust you will call on me. To me it has been a most inspiring experience."

In a December 15, 1953, letter to Mr. Taylor Spink of the *Sporting News*, Dr. Elkin said: "As Chairman of the Ty Cobb Foundation, I am very grateful to you for the publicity you gave it in the *Sporting News*, December 2." Then he asked for six copies of the magazine "for our files and some friends," enclosing a check for $1.50 to cover the costs.

He ended it by saying "I recall the World Series on one occasion with you and Ty when Happy (Chandler) was Commissioner and seeing you again at the Derby a moment. I trust our paths may cross again."

J. G. Taylor Spink, who was listed as the General Manager of the *Sporting News*, responded on December 19. "I was pleased to hear that you recalled the meeting I had with you when Happy was Commissioner and also when we met at the Derby. I, too, hope that our paths may cross again and I sincerely trust that if there is anything we can do in the way of publicity about the Memorial or otherwise, that you will advise us. My congratulations on the swell job you are doing."

Taylor Spink and Ty Cobb apparently were good

friends, and there is evidence in some publications that Spink spent some time with Cobb in his west coast homes.

The next letter from Ty Cobb to Dr. Elkin was dated December 9, 1953, and was addressed to "The Head 'Crovenay' #1." Webster's dictionary doesn't give us a meaning of the word "Crovenay" but it apparently was somewhat of a favorite joke between Ty Cobb and others, especially Dr. Elkin and Taylor Spink.

Spink, in an August 30, 1954, communication with Dr. Elkin also knew of the Crovenays. "Funny thing about the Crovenays and Ty," he wrote. "You know how he talks very quietly at times, especially when he asks me a question and often puts it in such a way, 'You remember...' I did not want to question the statement he made and said, 'Sure I do.' Then he promptly advised me, after a big laugh, that I had automatically become a member of the Crovenays. Quite a boy!"

As in many of Ty's letters, the December 9, 1953, scribbling in green ink, as was the most common case, jumped back and forth. It took him almost two pages to get him "to the real subject of this letter."

This photograph depicts the gold medallion that Ty Cobb presented to early Trustees, which is now in the possession of Mrs. Gwendolyn Caldwell, wife of the late Harmon W. Caldwell. Made of three kinds of gold, the medallion reads "HARMON W. CALDWELL - FOUNDER TRUSTEE - COBB EDUCATIONAL FOUNDATION" and includes a "tree of learning" and a lamp to "illumine the mind."

He was worried, it appears, that Dr. Elkin would have to spend too much time on the Ty Cobb Educational Fund, so he wanted him to "map out a plan" where requests could be answered with a form letter on how to proceed to qualify for a scholarship. "My desire is whatever you do or is to be done, I would like it to take a very minimum of your time."

For the first time, he mentioned that a stenographer or secretary would be needed to handle the details. "Eventually, it will come to this," he said.

He stated that the funds available would be $25,000

or more, enough to provide requirements for 18 to 20 students. "The board can govern the number chosen, etc. and control, of course, as to funds available," he said. "I would think your papers in Georgia would give this proper play, etc., where questions can be directed so you and others on the board will not be bothered with the details of such."

He also mentioned something about working with Trust Company Bank in drawing checks for scholarships. "I realize as now stands, certain steps should be taken so can you plan same and whatever you decide, go ahead?" *(See a copy of letter on pages 28-29.)*

As a side note, an attachment to the four-page letter asked Dr. Elkin to identify a man who had approached them at the Capitol City Club, asking Ty to come bird hunting at his place in Georgia. "He did not know what he was getting into," Ty wrote. "I might come in January. Give me his address and I will do the rest." *(See page 29.)*

Two days after writing the December 9 letter, Ty picked up his pen again for a December 11, 1953, offering. The logistics of setting up the Foundation obviously were heavy on his mind. He was interested in available funds, how many scholarships would be offered, letterheads, and as usual, the time all this was going to require of Dr. Elkin and others.

"I haven't gone over Trust setup as yet, but if no provision has been made for some available funds, then I will send check for what you all think [you] should have for any expense that comes up between this time and when larger amounts will be needed for students expense," he said.

He repeated that Dr. Elkin should find a stenographer to take care of any details "so as not to burden your time."

He talked about letterheads, cards outlining details for selections, and the number of scholarships to be offered. "Don't you think you should say there will be up to a certain number, possibly 18 or more, scholarships will be open?" he said. "Then, of course, Trustees can control the number selected." He felt that this would give students more of an incentive to apply, and that "they might not strive as they should" if they got the idea that only two or three scholarships were available.

"I expect to add each year to this initial fund," he pointed out. *(See a copy of the letter on pages 30-32.)*

Dr. Elkin and Dr. Caldwell were already at work on setting up the Foundation. In a December 16, 1953, letter to Cobb, Dr. Elkin wrote: "I have already given considerable thought and have consulted with Doctor Caldwell regarding the form for applications. I enclose a rough sketch of the scholarship application blank. Doctor Caldwell approved it also. There may be some minor changes before printing and I would like to have your opinion and that of Frances regarding it."

Dr. Elkin suggested that Cobb "forward to me the letters which you receive which I can have for my files." He said that he would answer all of them and give out information until the printed cards were ready.

"So far, some thirty or forty applications have come to me," he said, "mostly from high school students or their parents. All have been answered, giving the basic requirements for scholarship help and stating that the foundation has not been fully set up and will probably not be in operation until May."

He added that both he and Dr. Caldwell agreed that "we might make a slow start by picking out a few outstanding students who meet the requirements of the University of Georgia, Emory, and possibly Mercer, Agnes Scott, and Georgia Tech." He said that the Foundation could secure great help in screening these students from the Deans of these institutions.

"Letters of inquiry have been of little concern so far and my own secretarial staff has been glad to handle it," Dr. Elkin continued. "I think sometime in the future, however, it would be well to secure the part time services of a secretary who could handle this work after hours or on off days, possibly on an hourly basis. This I would estimate would not run more than $25.00 a month and I think stamps and printing could probably be included in that amount."

"Surely there is no need for a full time secretary," he concluded.

Thus, the Ty Cobb Educational Foundation was off and running!

A signed postcard of the original Cobb Memorial Hospital.

TYRUS R. COBB
48 SPENCER LANE, ATHERTON
MENLO PARK, CALIFORNIA

Nov - 10 - 53

Dear Doc:-

Yours of 6th Nov. received today,
note slow service on air mail service.
Note dates you can be in Atlanta and
the changes of from 6th to 18th and 25th to
Dec 1st, my time has little value and
have held myself to come there when
you can be free of ~~your~~ many
demands on your time.

I have everything ~~here~~ in readiness
and a talk with you + Dr. Caldwell
to o.k. everything, Truman Smith
can complete in a very short time
less than an hour as he has the
framework completed.

I have the medallions all completed,
and for some time.

Now if between, say 24th or 25th of Nov.
& Dec 1st will suit you, I will advise
exact date I will be there, I would
like to get it completed in 1953.

I have a friend who is head of

united press of quite a large zone
also high up as officer in
U.P. he wants to know when
so he can have his men there to
cover etc, the presentation etc.
publicity.

Frances left for Buffalo on 4th and
plans to meet me in Atlanta, she
has to act for her father in business
matters, they sold one of their places
means moving every thing also bought
a smaller place close to his offices etc.
and all the refinishing, painting,
changing she has to attend to.
As we get closer to the 23rd of Nov.
advise me if that period after is
open as per your letter of 6, then
I can contact Dr. Caldwell.
With kindest regards to Mrs. Elkin
and yourself, I am,
                              Sincerely

TYRUS R. COBB
48 SPENCER LANE, ATHERTON
MENLO PARK, CALIFORNIA

11/13/53

Dear Doc;-

Yours of 11/10/53 just recieved
and as you are I hasten to reply.
It is so rare to find one with the
fine quality of loyalty or the fineness
to remember so long a request, this
one doesnt see such in so many.
I feel honored you should have kept
in mind what I inquired of
and which you have informed
me of as a source which I could
apply to in securing some fine
old bourbon, I will say there is
no scent or smell that perfumes
the breath of man as good and
"old" bourbon, paints landscapes
on ones brain, adds impulses
also creates thoughts which hastens
expressions in words bey ond ones
normal capacity, I am sorry I
cannot now follow up your message
and information to me, very
important and possibly most, is
that following a different regimen,

20

have for some time but not necessarily, all the way in this life but confess I have toyed with this idea, No not the doctors just I myself elected my present practice, I might add and confess, for my very deep love for Frances and strange silence and expressions, no protests, I decided what it was and put my plan into effect some time ago, I did rule out, at my discretion, unusual situations possibly a token drink so far this rule has not been resorted to.

Now after the above comes the price subject with the holding so long of this priceless fluid and interest costs computed the price asked no doubt is in line, but it seems in the general price range of so called Napoleon brandy which has been for years so proposed, for no doubt little if any exists today, if a few bottles then they are museum pieces in some of the old and famous connoisseurs or collectors cellars.

I am not a connoisseur and can not be a collector, besides my curiosity would get the best of me and I would break my pledge Etc. Your letter "to ask them to save it for me or merely to look in on them the next time I am in N.y." you give me a thought, possibly I shall to to the "house of Lehmann" and satisfy myself by just looking at this fine and old bourbon. Enough of this.

I am happy to know you will be available between 2x th & Dec 2nd it fits into my plans perfectly, first Frances might not be completed in her duties in Buffalo, N.Y. and am sure she will by last week in Nov. and can join me there in Atlanta, if she finishes earlier she may come home and then with me to Atlanta Etc.

I have an invitation in St. Louis Mo. a friend being honored Dec 23rd, Nashville Banner wanted me to come for their 50th anniversary some few months ago, I could not, so they asked if I could come at any time later, I have written them and asked could I come around 2x of Nov. will hear soon, so I should plan safely to be in Atlanta on 25th or 26th, so if you can say for sure any date between 2x th and say 28th also the Dr. Caldwell then you set the date and write me so I can make permanent, my plans.

As before stated I am ready.

I planned on Johnson, lawyer of Royston, more of a friendly gesture honor to him Etc, very small town people are so very slow, he was 2½ months answering a letter asking information of him, I wrote him back at once to handle the matter of paintings of my mother and father also myself which should have a proper placement, I asked him as trustee to effect this for diplomatically reasons as the illustrious widow of Dr. Brown had usurped the proper place in the Cobb Memorial Hospital by hanging a rather small and not at all well done painting or not sure whether it was one of those blown up photographs with an oil covering to resemble a painting also a man skelton who helped oversee the building work, both there, in the place, I asked Johnson to handle the matter, in trustee meeting or in person, havent heard from him thats as I said some my request about painting was not less than 3 months ago, the Cobb paintings are hung in another place, as I have had a relative go there and see and report back so I knew, which all means I have changed my mind as to Johnson's being a trustee with yourself & Dr. Caldwell, now I ask you do we need or have to have a third member and if so please be thinking of a proper person that will serve, I have Johnsons medalion with name finished and complete but I have been to the jewelers here and they have assured me they can remove Johnson's name and put on another Etc.

Do please pardon the infliction of such a long letter also such details, but I have to give you the picture.

In closing, I hope all will go off properly, think a good idea to have press & news services on hand for the short ceremony of presentations and announcement I have revealed my intent to some and they want to be there also promised there would me no abortive announcement and of course if we keep date secret they would not announce anyhow, the short ceremony can be done any where, hotel, club or any place you elect as best, we can have a luncheon, and is understood now same, no other way. I am to host same, no other way would say, presentations, announcements, you, pictures, finish, except luncheon.

I would like a day at least to complete matters with Trust Co. of Georgia and Truman Smith also a meeting with Trustees for a talk of plans so 27th or 28th of Nov. would dove tail my plans.

Let me hear from you as soon as you can so I can advise Smith of my date to see him also about Dr. Caldwell and your suggestion as to third trustee if we have to have a third.

I am,

Sincerely

Ty

written but not re-read. ha!

23

Atlanta, Ga.

Ty Cobb, whose record as the game's greatest player has been immortalized in the Hall of Fame, made a lasting contribution to another field in which he is interested, when he announced the establishment of the Cobb Educational Foundation to help qualified students continue their college educations.

In making the announcement here, November 27, the Georgia Peach presented handsome gold medallions to Dr. Dan C.Elkin, professor of medicine and head of the medical department of Emory University,Atlanta, and Dr.Harmon Caldwell, head of all higher educational institutions in Georgia, who will serve, along with either Cobb or his wife, as trustees of the foundation.

"For a long time, I have been interested in doing something along educational lines," Cobb said. His father, William H.Cobb, was active in educational matters and, as a Georgia state senator, worked for improved schools and higher pay for teaching personnel. He was the first man in the country to evolve the idea of consolidating rural schools, in 1902, and crusaded for the plan of combining "little red schoolhouses" to provide better educational facilities.

The Cobb Educational Foundation will select deserving applicants, after their freshman year in college, and will aid them financially through the completion of their studies. The trustees will decide on the recipients on the basis of the students' records and after personal interviews. Both boys and girls will be eligible for the assistance and their field of study will not be restricted.

"Naturally, they will be limited in number to fit my purse in donations," Cobb explained. He plans to make yearly contributions to the foundation. In preparing for the project, he said,"for three years, all the fees that I was fortunate enough to receive from magazines, radio, TV, testimonials, etc., have been earmarked for the fund."

Cobb, who now resides in San Francisco, made a special trip to his native state to announce his benefaction.

December 17, 1953

Mr. Joseph T. Nolan
Sunday Department
The New York Times
Times Square
New York, N. Y.

Dear Mr. Nolan:

        I am in receipt of your letter regarding the Cobb Educational Foundation which was set up by Mr. Cobb this year. In answer to your questions:

1. Money has been provided by Mr. Cobb and turned over to the Trust Company of Georgia as trustees. The income of this fund will be used for scholarships. The amount of the fund has not been announced, nor will it be, but I can say that it will give partial aid each year to some eight to twenty students, depending upon the available funds and the need of scholarship aid in individual cases.

2. Scholarships are open to residents of Georgia who have finished at least the Freshman year in an accredited college.

3. Scholarships are available for higher education either academic, professional or technological.

4. Students will be chosen after investigation as to their needs, scholarship, ability, integrity, and personality.

5. They will be chosen by a Board of Trustees which is self perpetuating. At the present time it is composed of:

    1. Doctor Daniel C. Elkin, Professor of Surgery, Emory University Hospital, Emory University, Georgia, Chairman.

    2. Doctor Harmon Caldwell, Chancellor of the University of Georgia.

    3. Mrs. Tyrus R. Cobb, wife of the donor.

    4. Doctor Fred W. Rankin, Lexington, Kentucky. President of the American College of Surgeons and past President of the American Medical Association.

6. The scholarship funds are outright gifts and not loans but will only partly cover the students expenses.

7. Mr. Cobb will play no active part in the choosing of students although he will certainly take an active interest in their careers and will undoubtedly make every effort to know them personally.

8. You pose a difficult question as to how he became interested. Mr. Cobb has been fortunate in his investments and, as you probably know, is an extremely keen and active man. His own education stopped at the end of High School and he has always felt that he missed something, I have heard him express this on numerous occasions, in not going to college. His father was a college graduate, a well educated man. He was Superintendent of the schools of Franklin County, Georgia, and as a member of the Georgia State Senate he was primarily interested in promoting educational facilities, particularly in raising the pay for teachers and in the consolidation of rural schools, in which he took a lead. Mr. Cobb is a sentimentalist and has a great feeling for his family. On this account he built a hospital at Royston, Georgia, in memory of his father and mother. This has been in successful operation since 1951.

I believe it was in 1904, when Mr. Cobb was seventeen years old and when he had a local High School record as a baseball player, that he made the decision to try out for professional baseball. Meanwhile his father had entered him at the University of Georgia. At that time the South Athletic League was organized and Ty wrote to each of eight clubs asking for a try out. Only Augusta responded and they told him that he could try out at his own expense. Then came the question of breaking the news to his father, and after an all night session the old man gave in at 3:00 A. M. and Ty made off for Augusta, trying out as an utility infielder. It so happened that the first baseman became ill and since there were but few players, the center fielder was moved to first and Ty got a chance in the out field where he played two games, making three hits and stealing two bases. The first baseman then recovered and Ty was released. He played that summer in a semiprofessional league at Anniston, Alabama. During this time he would slip into drug stores, furniture stores, and other business establishments and use their stationery in writing anonymous letters to Grantland Rice, then with the Atlanta Journal, extolling the virtues of this young Cobb. Rice finally took some notice of this avalanche of recommendations and Augusta recalled him and, I believe, he played there about a month when he was bought by Detroit for $500 plus a $200 bonus for reporting late that season. You know the rest of the story.

I might add that all the money which he has received from newspaper and magazine articles and testimonials has been kept separate for this fund and to it he has also added, and will continue to add, from his private resources.

The Atlanta Constitution of Saturday, November 28th, carried an article by Furman Bisher, Sports Editor of the Constitution, which is informative and fairly accurate and the Atlanta Journal-Constitution of Sunday, November 29th, carried a column by Ralph McGill, Editor of the Atlanta Constitution. Both of these may be of some help to you in this story.

26

I might add that Ty has gone into this matter after considerable thoght and consultation and that his wife has been an eager helpmate in his deliberations. He has no delusions about the ability of the trustees to pick outstanding people because he has said to me on numerous occasions, "If we can pick one winner before I die, I will think the project worth-while. I have seen too many well advertised boys come to training camp who never made the big leagues and I doubt one in fifty of the yearlings sold at Keenland and Saratoga ever win a stake."

At a press conference he was asked if these were athletic scholarships and he replied, "No." A reporter then asked him to expand on this and he rather laconically said, "Absolutely no."

Cobb still maintains a keen interest in sports but he reads widely and well and has an excellent education. He much prefers to talk upon subjects of general interest rather than sports, although at times he can tell wonderful stories of his athletic career. He writes long and interesting letters regarding his trips and regarding his philanthropies, but only to intimate friends who have some interest in his projects, and I might add that in the numerous letters which I have received from him I have never seen a grammatical error and he has no secretary like you and I to pick up his mistakes.

I hope I have been of some help to you in this story. If I can be of further help I trust you will call on me. To me it has been a most inspiring experience. You may reach me at this address or should you desire to call me the telephone number is CR 5377, or home phone AT 2410.

Sincerely yours,

D. C. Elkin, M. D.

DCE:alf

Encl. 2

TYRUS R. COBB
48 SPENCER LANE, ATHERTON
MENLO PARK, CALIFORNIA 12/9/53

The "Head" "Crovenay" # 1 :—
familiarity of salution, Please pardon this
laughs could be drab also. note I
have a strictly personal on envelope.
We are back home as you see,
last night seven forty P.M. in
Mexico City 12 oclock noon their
time here at above time (here).
We had a most interesting trip,
saw much of interest in the
short time & without rush, really
the antiquity and civilization back
long ago, impresses one so much.
Met some southern people living
down there which was very
refreshing after so much of
the mexican etc.
Received your post card from
Chicago, thanks for the thought
and honor re Crovenay.
Our hotel "Bamer" a new one and
really fine, there met Gary Cooper
my first time, in my mind I

was much tempted to try to qualify myself in reaching the position of a "Croneay" but he scared me off, he was so laconic, he seemed to me to be a natural and if I had been successful I would now have been making my report to you for acceptance in the charmed circle, instead I can only report I find several "phoney" letters about the qualifying for the Educational Fund, some cannot spell, some out of state also those who want contributions for some cause, these, have been accustomed to in past, which brings me to the real subject of this letter, Only when you have time and can, map out a plan, where letters can be received, a form letter answering also outling outlining aims Etc. and how all are to proceed to qualify, there will be need for stationery and also expense

incurred, in time, when convenient rough a plan out to this end, you and Dr. Caldwell know just what and how to do this, my desire is whatever you do or is to be done, I would like it to take a very minimum of your time, have a set up where it will work automatically some stenographer or secretary to handle the details, with recompense Etc, eventually it will come to this.
The funds available will be $25000⁰⁰ or some more, already stock I put up has enhanced, an announcement to papers there as to the approximate number of applicants that could be successful in fulfilling requirements could be 18 or 20, as I am to put in a sum each year, the board can govern the number chosen Etc. and control of course as to funds available, then outline what will be required in the prospective applicants, and of course their need for the aid Etc. I would think your papers in Georgia would give all this the proper play Etc.

also where any questions can be directed so you and others on the board will not be bothered with the details of such.
I have received something from Trust Company there also Frances as a trustee and was understood same should go to you and rest of trustees, now the funds must be made available for any use of trustees, so the Trust Co. should set this up with proper power to draw checks on, of course for students will be later but now expense Etc. will be needed.
I hope you will bear with me in this, I realize as now stands, certain steps should be taken, so can you plan same and whatever you decide, go ahead?
I know of all this infliction and hope you will forgive me. We are well & fine, also Frances joins me in very best to Mrs. Elkins & yourself. Sincerely Ty

Doc:-
who was the man who came to your table at Capital City club and asked me to come bird hunting on his place in Georgia, for he did not know what he was getting into — I might come in January Give me his address and I will do the rest.

— Ty —

12/11/53

Dear Doc:-

I haven't gone over Trust set up as yet but if no provision at this time has been made for some available funds to check on as deposited then I will send check for what you all think should have for any expense that comes up between this time and when larger amounts will be needed for students expense is started or some provision made to sign a note with Trust cov in name of Educational fund with the 250 shares of Coca cola stock they have as security etc. the idea is not to sell coca cola stock now, but to hold as it no doubt will enhance in value materially also dividends, holding the stock and making notes for money use when needed seems to be a good plan, I wrote yesterday on some stenographer to take care of any details, also stamp & other expense so as not to burden your time.

Now I want your ideas and

approval on this, I would like to
have a die made, a replica
of medallions to Trustees, for
letter heads and a card,
outlining details of selections
to be made (students, freshmen class,
any college at discretion of Trustees
all expense of college or 3/4 or
whatever you trustees decide as
best, also its possible students might
feel there will only be two or
three scholarships, don't you think
you should say there will be up
to a certain number possibly 18 or more
scholarships will be open, then
of course Trustees can control the
number selected, this will give
students more of an incentive
when if they might get the idea of
only two or three scholarships,
they might not strive as they should,
I expect to add each year to
this initial fund.
If you with ideas of Dr. Rankin & Dr.
Caldwell can condense all relative
to the plan, requirements, selection, students
to come from Georgia institutions or

citizens of Georgia (again whatever you Trustees think best) this to go on a card or one page to fold to fit the regular envelope to be used. send to me with any instructions or directions, I will have a die made also stationery & cards finished and send to you, which will cut down, letter answering, there will be serious questioning about this plan also many "bug" letters, I have some already, in the above way these can be handled without much work.

Yes and instruct me as to letter heading Educational Fund Etc. also trustees, a sketch by sending details to a stationer there and they arrange for balance Etc. Or better still, I will have the die made here and printing can be made done in Atlanta.

I hope in this confused and garbled letter, you can gain what I am trying for, to relieve you of as much your time as I can. There is no intent to rush, you are to decide when you want this done.

as Ever
— R —

I am,

CHAPTER THREE

The Fund

You are doubtless familiar with the Educational Fund which Mr. Tyrus R. Cobb has just established. The agreement itself was signed on November 30 and 250 shares of Coca-Cola common stock delivered to us as Trustee, to constitute the original Trust Fund.

— Letter dated December 2, 1953, from Carroll Payne Jones, Trust Officer for Trust Company of Georgia, to Foundation Trustees Mrs. Tyrus R. Cobb, Dr. Daniel C. Elkin, Dr. Harmon Caldwell and Dr. Fred W. Rankin

When Tyrus R. Cobb established the Ty Cobb Educational Foundation in late 1953, he left no stones unturned. His friend Furman Smith, an Atlanta attorney with King & Spalding, worked with Carroll Payne Jones, Trust Officer with Trust Company of Georgia, in writing the legal document for the scholarship fund.

"For the purpose of creating a permanent educational fund to be known as the "TY COBB EDUCATION-AL FUND", I, TYRUS R. COBB, have transferred and delivered and do hereby transfer, assign and convey to TRUST COMPANY OF GEORGIA (hereinafter called the Trustee), as Trustee, the property shown on the schedule hereto attached and made a part hereof, in trust for the following uses and purposes," the official document begins.

"Item I" of the Charter provided that "Said Trustee shall manage, invest and reinvest said fund as the Ty Cobb Educational Fund to provide for the manual arts school, technological, professional, or college education of qualified boys and girls who otherwise would be unable to secure such education."

"Item II" established the Scholarship Board "consisting originally of Dr. Daniel C. Elkin, Dr. Harmon Caldwell, Dr. Fred W. Rankin, and Mrs. Tyrus R. Cobb." The document points out that "In all matters a decision of a majority of said Board shall control and the Trustees shall be authorized to act on any paper signed by a majority of the Board as constituting the act of the Board." Further, it instructs remaining board members to name successors, should a vacancy occur, and that the new members would "have all the rights, powers and duties of the original board members." And, even further, it appoints the judge of the Superior Court of Franklin County, Georgia, to fill vacancies, in the event remaining members fail to act.

"Item III" calls for the Trustee to advise the Scholarship Board from time to time, and at least annually, of the income on hand and of the amount of income reasonably expected. It specifies that the Scholarship Board shall then advise the Trustee in writing of the persons to whom scholarships are awarded and the amount of such scholarships. The Trustee, according to the Charter, then would make payment to the recipients.

"Item IV" is a notation from Cobb himself. "It is my intention to add to this fund from time to time until the value of the fund is at least $150,000 and any funds or property added to this fund shall be held by the Trustee in all respects as if it had originally been a part of this fund." He continued: "It is my hope that this fund will constitute a permanent fund that eventually the income only will be used for scholarships. However, I realize that during the first few years until the income is sufficient to provide one or more scholarships, it will be necessary for the Scholarship Board to use principal for the purpose of providing scholarships."

"Item V" provides the Trustee with powers to sell, exchange and invest property, stocks, bonds, securities of other investments.

"Item VI" provides that the Trustee must furnish the Scholarship Board, "and to me as long as I am in life," a statement of the assets held by the Trustee and of its receipts and disbursements.

"Item VII" covers the possibility of Trust Company of Georgia merging or consolidating with another bank or trust company.

"Item VIII" covers compensation for the Trustee, before and after the death of Ty Cobb.

"IN WITNESS WHEREOF, I have hereunto set my hand and affixed my seal and the Trustee, to evidence its acceptance of the trust herein created, has caused this instrument to be signed by its duly authorized officer this 30th day of November, 1953."

– signed by Tyrus R. Cobb, the Grantor, and Carroll Payne Jones, Trust Officer for Trust Company of Georgia, Trustee

– signed, sealed and delivered in the presence of Furman Smith and Eugenia H. Brook, Notary Public

– approved as to form by Furman Smith, counsel for Grantor

– filed in the State of Georgia, County of Fulton

In the December 2, 1953, letter from Trust Company of Georgia, referred to at the outset of this chapter, Mr. Carroll Payne Jones expanded on the original investment of 250 shares of Coca-Cola common stock.

"Since the Coca-Cola shares will not be transferred to the Trust in time to control the December dividend, the first income expected by the Fund will be on April 1 of next year," he pointed out. "At that time, if the Coca-Cola Company pays the expected dividend of $1.00 per share, the Fund will have its first income of $250.00. As you will note from the agreement, however, Mr. Cobb expects to add to this Fund from time to time."

The files of the Foundation reveal a "principal statement" from Trust Company of Georgia as of October 20, 1954, reflecting the book value of the 250 shares of Coca-Cola stock at $27,312.50. The second page of the statement reveals the expenditures of the first six scholarships, totaling $2,900.00, and receipts in the amount of $3,075.07; leaving a balance of $175.07 in the receipt column. The third page revealed dividends of $250.00 on July 2 and $250.00 on October 4, adding to the $175.07 and providing an increase of $669.57 and increasing the value of the Foundation to $27,982.07.

No mention is made of a possible $250.00 on April 1 or where the $3,075.07 came from to fund the initial scholarships.

But, in another file, a December 11, 1953, letter from Ty Cobb to Dr. Daniel Elkin, the Chairman, revealed that there were early concerns over start-up money.

"I haven't gone over Trust setup as yet, but if no provision at this time has been made for some available funds to check on as deposited, then I will send check for what you all think [you] should have for any expense that comes up between this time and when larger amounts will be needed for students expense is started, or some provision made to sign a note with Trust Co. in name of Educational Fund with the 250 shares of Coca Cola stock they have as security," he said in a lengthy start to a three-page letter. He added: "I wrote yesterday for some stenographer to take care of any details, also start-up and other expense, so as not to burden your time." *(See copy of letter in Chapter 2 - Getting Started, pages 30-32.)*

The paper trail in the Foundation files all but disappeared for several months after the November and December 1953 beginnings. Little, if anything, was documented about that first meeting, held during the summer of 1954, until an August 16, 1954, "Press Release to Mr. Brad Ansley" appeared from the Office of Dr. Daniel C. Elkin, chairman of the Cobb

Educational Foundation.

The first class of scholarship winners were announced, including Mr. James Allen Butts of Blairsville, a sophomore at Emory University; Mr. Eugene Ralston Griffith of Atlanta, a senior at Virginia Military Institute; Miss Barbara Evelyn Sherwood of Atlanta, a sophomore at Piedmont College; Mr. David Clayton Smisson of Fort Valley, a graduate of The Citadel and a freshman at Johns Hopkins School of Medicine in Baltimore; Mr. Charles Kenneth Butterworth of Canton, a sophomore at North Georgia College; and Mr. Oscar Newton Maxwell, Jr. of Macon, a senior at Mercer University.

Cobb and one of his dogs.

"The six scholarships being awarded for the approaching school year," the release stated, "are the first derived from the trust fund established by Mr. Tyrus R. Cobb to provide for college educations of qualified boys and girls who otherwise would be unable to secure such educations.

"Provisions of the Foundation stipulate that scholarship winners must be residents of the state of Georgia and must have completed at least their freshman year's work in an accredited school or university.

"Announcement of the scholarship winners is made by Dr. Daniel C. Elkin, Chairman of the Board of Trustees; Mrs. Tyrus R. Cobb and Dr. Harmon Caldwell, Trustees."

Four days later, on August 20, 1954, Alice Merchant, secretary to Dr. Elkin, wrote to Mr. and Mrs. Cobb at their home in Douglas County, Nevada. "I am enclosing sample copies of Dr. Elkin's recent letters to students in connection with the awarding of the scholarships for this year," she wrote. "I am also enclosing a clipping from *The Atlanta Journal* announcing the awards. As is the usual difficulty with a press release, all the information supplied was not used, and it was particularly regrettable to both Dr. Elkin and me that the names of Mrs. Cobb and Dr. Caldwell were not included with Dr. Elkin's as announcing the awards."

"The Trust Company of Georgia has already issued the checks to cover the scholarship grants for each of the six students, the checks having been forwarded directly to the treasurers of the schools involved," she added.

The above communication is the only mention of that first meeting where scholarships were awarded.

Now, it's pretty obvious that Ty Cobb loved to write long and sentimental letters, especially to Dr. Elkin in the early years and later to Miss Carroll McMahon, the Foundation's second secretary. It's unlikely that there was no communication between Cobb and Dr. Elkin during early 1954, but for some unknown reason, there is no file of would-be letters.

But, in August, 1954, it started all over again.

A juicy six-pager, dated August 21, 1954, came to "Dear Doc" with perhaps more information than the good doctor wanted to know. *(See copy of letter on pages 57-59.)*

Cobb talked about entertaining some "kids" with ice cream and that he liked the idea of "Hap" (Governor A. B. "Happy" Chandler of Kentucky), who apparently was being proposed to join the Board of Trustees of the Foundation. He rambled about a personal run-in with the law, advising Dr. Elkin that if he should ever be driving that way to remember Placerville, CA.

"Don't go there," he said.

He mentioned that Taylor Spinks (of *Sports Illustrated*) was coming for a visit and that he had hoped to have him there at the same time Dr. and Mrs. Elkin had visited. Then, he mentioned something about the "Crovenay fish platter" and about photos of the Elkins from the trip. "I don't know if you are Crovenay Elkin or Crovenay Sherlock Holmes with that sporting cap you had on," Ty joked.

Later in the letter he reported that he had received a "very nice letter from Butts, Blairsville, Georgia, which am enclosing." James Butts was one of the original scholars named by the Foundation. "He makes certain avowals and am feeling sure he will not have to be prompted by the Trustees," Ty said.

Cobb's "Aunt Nora" from North Carolina had visited with young Butts and found him "working" in the field. "I think that is great," he concluded.

Finally, he asked Dr. Elkin to have his secretary contact each student and ask them for a picture. "I would like to keep an album as I enjoy sizing them up and "Doc" they do look good & fine as types."

Nine days later (August 30, 1954), Cobb's pen struck again. Along with it, he enclosed a letter from a "Mr. Candler" dealing again with James Butts, "your first choice." He obviously was responding to a letter from Dr. Elkin, agreeing with him "so heartily" about some subject and talking about the nice letters he had received from several of the students. "Appreciations that sound so sincere and determined as to their efforts, etc.," he said. *(See copy of letter on pages 60-63.)*

And again, Cobb popped what was to be a continuing request. "I am not prompting," he said, "I know you are busy and no doubt the matter is already taken care of, but I do want the pictures of these who qualified."

Then he switched to money. "I wrote you about, when you needed proper funds, cash to be used as Coca-Cola stock is not to be sold now," he said. "I earned $500 the other day, which goes to fund, except it will go as equivalent in stock which when sold, no capital gains tax, etc."

Next came a long dissertation about this "Aunt Nora" who was introduced in the previous letter. "Aunt Nora is quite a person, a true Cobb (you will pardon my briefing you)," he wrote. He suggested that she probably already had made contact with Dr. Elkin, possibly asking for funds for a student near her North Carolina home. "Aunt Nora in her enthusiasm wants to break state lines per our set up and include the Cobb home county which is in North Carolina by a very short distance," he said. "She wants to bend the state line. She has written me so."

Then, he drew a straight line. "As you know this

should not be done, to change the set up, so you tell her, the set up and cannot be deviated from."

Yet another letter, this one dated September 4, 1954, arrived for Dear "Doc" a short time later. *(See copy of letter on pages 64-65.)* Included was a letter from "a friend who is to my estimation a modest and unsung genius, a real sincere fellow." This friend, Earl Bell, was pleading the case of his son for a scholarship.

"Earl has no resources and here I say I am in no way pleading his case," Cobb wrote. "Every person must qualify with the Board of Trustees...do not judge or give his son any consideration beyond what you give others." Later, he added: "I shall never in any way try to influence. Judge the boy severely but let Earl Bell know I have done my part on [a] friendship basis."

Then he added "I am so pleased 'Happy' has accepted...he will be a good one," having heard through some means that Happy Chandler had agreed to join the Trustees. In addition, he suggested that "Bob Jones" be considered for the board, adding that "I think it a crime the democrats used the rotten methods to one of the most perfect gentleman I have ever known." The "crime" is not noted, but the person referred to could have been the great Bobby Jones, with whom Ty had played a great deal of golf through the years.

From the letter, Jones obviously was connected with Coca-Cola, which kicked off the next subject in Cobb's early September 1954 letter. "Coca-Cola [stock] is drifting down and for no reason," he wrote, "per terrific surplus, also no split...since 1935."

Later he said the he had some cash that could be used to buy stock. "I then could use some of my old and cheap Coke stock to place for [the] Educational Fund," he wrote. "I would like to buy some more Coke, purpose as explained."

Then he suggested that Dr. Elkin do some checking on 'Coke.' "Now no one can come out cold turkey and say so-and-so except R.W.W. (Robert W. Woodruff of Coca-Cola), but I thought possibly Smith (his lawyer) or Jones of Trust Department might give the news only by a hint that Coke operations was [sic] normal or say well no one should sell now."

Apologizing for asking Dr. Elkin to check, he concluded that "I would like to buy a few hundred more shares so I can release a little amount of some stock bought cheap to Educational Fund, but I want to be sure there has been nothing drastic affecting 'Coke' this year."

In addition to giving money out of his pocket (or in stocks), Ty Cobb provided contributions to the Educational Fund in a number of other ways. He would make speeches or testimonials and donate the money to the Fund.

In late 1954, he was contacted by a small-business man from Atlanta who wanted to use Cobb's name and picture to promote his product. Robert Glenn Manufacturing Co. was a small company that made table slides, a gadget which you put under the table to assist the housewife in putting in extra leaves when company comes. Mr. Glenn wanted to use as his slogan, "The Greatest Slide Since Ty Cobb" and wanted to use Cobb's picture on a calendar.

Writing to Cobb at the baseball greats Nevada home, Glenn asked for the "privilege of using your name in our business slogan." Cobb had agreed to allow the company to use his name "at no charge" but when Glenn added the part about the picture, Cobb decided a $1,000 fee would be in order.

In a September 8, 1954, letter to Dr. Daniel C. Elkin, Chairman of the Educational Fund, Cobb wrote: "I am enclosing a letter from one of your commercial fellow townsman, one Robert Glenn. He says he has a hell of a business. He wrote me, he called me, and I agreed to let him use the slogan 'The Greatest Slide Since Ty Cobb,' no charge. Now, as you can see, he wants to dig deeper and wants my picture, etc."

He asked "Doc" to "ring this fellow up" and to tell him, that since he is doing a big business "we will accept $1,000.00" for the Educational Fund. *(See copy of letter on pages 66-67.)*

Dr. Elkin did meet with Glenn and told him about the Fund, and suggested to Cobb that he go ahead with a contract.

Promotional postcard for Robert Glenn MFG.Co.

So on September 27 Glenn wrote to Ty Cobb.

"Dear Mr. Cobb: Thank you for your letter of the 22nd. I want you to know that what you are doing is a great benefit to our state and country because our young people certainly need an education to carry on our cherished traditions that are fast becoming demolished." Later in the letter he offered: "I should like to pay you $50.00 per month toward the great program you have created for the school children. That will be $600.00 per year. Suppose we do this for a three-year contract and if our business grows and merits more, then at the end of three years we will increase our offer." *(see letter on page 70.)*

To which Cobb responded to Dr. Elkin in a October 2, 1954, letter:

"Dear 'Doc': - Enclosed [you] will find [a] letter from Glenn of Atlanta. He is pledged to $50.00 per month for three years and he might grow. No doubt he is small, and besides, he could have had it for some time for only $1,000.00. This way, we can be assured the money he pays will take care of possibly three, but one for each year for three years." Cobb concluded in a P.S. that the funds would come to him "so I can get credit income tax and I will donate stock to fund."

Cobb also suggested for Dr. Elkin to "'put the works' to him (Glenn) for more 'if' you can. I will ask him to call you and come to see you so 'take' care of him for as much as you can, for we want to school some boys or girls." *(See copy of letter on pages 68-69.)*

On the bottom of Mr. Glenn's letter to Cobb, Ty scribbled: "P.S. Get him up higher if [you] can but close with him on what you deem fit. Show him the boys records, etc." *(See page 70 for Glenn's letter.)*

There are no records of contributions in the files, but if it worked, the Educational Fund certainly came away with an early boost in revenues. And, there is no record of whether Dr. Elkin was able to, or wanted to "put the works" to Glenn for more money.

Apparently, money did not flow into the Fund in the beginning as Cobb and Dr. Elkin had hoped. Reflective of this was a December 20, 1954, letter from Dr. Elkin to Mrs. Ty Cobb in her Atherton home in Menlo Park, California.

"We now have $750.00 in cash in the bank with a prospect of some $1,400.00 more if Coca-Cola pays its dividend," Dr. Elkin wrote. "I am sure that you and Ty would like to give ten scholarships of $500.00 each; therefore, we need some money. This is putting the matter on a commercial basis."

Dr. Elkin noted in the letter that as of January first, Miss Merchant would write to the six colleges where students received the initial scholarships in 1954, making inquiries regarding the progress of the scholars. "I think the reports will be good because they were selected with great care and, moreover, I think they should be continued because all of them are certainly needy students," he wrote.

"I have tried as best I could to keep this out of Emory and out of medical education feeling that there were other things that were just as important," he continued. "However, it looks like everybody wants to be a doctor nowadays.

"One of these boys is now at Hopkins, as you know, one is going to the University of Georgia, and one is at Emory," the letter from Dr. Elkin to Mrs. Cobb said. "There happens to be a very good girl here who needs the money and wants to go to medical school; in fact, she has been admitted. I hesitate to ask her to make application and then turn her down."

The Cobb files went blank again for the first part of 1955 until a July 12, 1955, letter from Alice Merchant was mailed to Mr. and Mrs. Cobb. "Dr. Elkin advised me some time ago of your plans to be in Atlanta around the 20th of July," she wrote. "I have a complete file for your records of the students whom the scholarships were awarded last year as I understand Mrs. Cobb wants to keep a scrapbook about these young students. I have made copies of our correspondence with them during the year, and their letters alone would reassure you that the establishment of the Cobb Educational Foundation was no mistake."

She noted that earlier in the spring she had written each of the Georgia colleges soliciting applications and that 60 had been received, including renewal applica-

tions from each of the previous year's scholarship winners. "All of our students have done excellent work this year," she concluded, "and I think it will be a real satisfaction to you to see their records."

Eleven awards – four renewals and seven new awards – were approved for the 1955-56 school year. A total of $5,500 was awarded during the second annual meeting of the Fund's Trustees, held on July 21, 1955.

Records show that Cobb provided a check in the amount of $10,000 on July 22, 1955, just in time for the Foundation's second set of scholarships.

Included among the renewals were Eugene Griffith (UGA Medical School), James Butts (Emory University), David Smisson (Johns Hopkins University), and Charles Butterworth (North Georgia College). And, incidentally, there was not a new award made to a student at Emory's medical school, indicating that Dr. Elkin did not, in fact, encourage that "very good girl here" to apply.

Announcement of the scholarship winners was made by Trustees of the Foundation – Dr. Elkin, Mrs. Cobb, Dr. Caldwell, and Mr. A. B. "Happy" Chandler of Versailles, Kentucky. Also attending the meeting was Dean Prentice Miller of Emory University's Lower Division who years later would become Chairman of the Trustees, and Mr. J. B. Richner of Trust Company of Georgia.

In a July 23, 1955, letter to Mr. Clark Howell of *The Atlanta Constitution*, Dr. Elkin requested a "small editorial" regarding the Cobb Foundation. "Some way the rumor got out that there was more smoke than fire, which is entirely untrue as may be seen by the fact that we gave out eleven scholarships this year," the letter stated.

"Ty, like most professional athletes, is a sensitive, neurotic soul, and a little praise would stimulate him to even more generosity," he concluded. The news report, he added, appeared in the previous day's "Mullet Wrapper."

Interestingly, on July 30, 1955, Dr. Elkin received a letter from Taylor Spink of the *Sporting News* who had written *The Constitution* for authority to reprint the editorial from the July 26 issue entitled "Ty Cobb Foundation Is Boon to Georgia Youth." Spink also included a tear sheet from the *Sporting News* showing reference to the awards already made.

"I have not heard from Ty for some time," Spink said. "He had been in touch with me in connection with making a trip to Cooperstown (and the Hall of Fame).

It was utterly impossible for me to get away, and I am sorry that he may have felt that I was not mindful of his invitation. If I had five or ten million dollars worth of Coca-Cola stock, I could travel around the country in a private car!"

In a September 2, 1955, letter to Ty Cobb, Miss Merchant related that she was still waiting for another student photo before sending him the complete files for the 1955-56 year. "I think this will be a good way for us to preserve the history of the Cobb Foundation, and I am anxious that you have them to read over for yourself," she said.

"The little boy we had selected who wanted to study veterinary medicine wrote me such a nice letter," she continued. "He had thought he was going to have to give up his ambition and settle on another profession which would take less schooling. That once instance alone should make us all realize that the Cobb Foundation is a great thing."

Then, on September 7th she wrote Ty Cobb again.

"No doubt by this date you have received a copy of the Ralph McGill editorial which appeared in *The Atlanta Constitution* on September 3rd," she said. "I have obtained copies for each of our 11 scholars and I know that each one will treasure this little write-up about 'the best player of all time.' "

"I have through my letters attempted to impress on the children the very sincere personal feeling you have about each of them," she continued, "and I know this article will but further emphasize the fact to them and inspire each of them."

Jumping ahead yet another year, the Foundation files reveal that the third group of scholarships was awarded at a June 30, 1956, meeting in Atlanta. An expanded Board of Trustees included Dr. Elkin, now professor emeritus of Emory University, as chairman; Chancellor Harmon W. Caldwell of the University System of Georgia; Honorable A. B. Chandler, governor of the State of Kentucky; Mr. Earle Combs of Richmond, Kentucky, a baseball great who years later would be

Honorary coaches Babe Ruth and Ty Cobb at the youth all star game in 1945.

named to the Hall of Fame; Dr. Charles S. Kennedy of Detroit, Michigan, a member of the Board of Regents at the University of Michigan; and Mr. Tyrus R. Cobb.

A then-record 23 scholarships – 9 renewals and 14 new awards – were granted for the 1956-57 year, an expenditure of $8,900.00.

Miss Carroll McMahon, secretary to Dr. Caldwell at the Board of Regents, had taken over duties as Secretary of the Foundation in February 1956 and thus was working her first annual meeting with the Board of Trustees.

Most of the letters in the Foundation file from this point (1956) until the end of Cobb's life (1961) were addressed to "Dear Miss McMahon" as was the one dated July 26, 1956. The secretary apparently had mailed Cobb information about the 1956-57 awards.

"I want to acknowledge receipt of and thank you for your thought and kindness in sending me the material you did relative to the students who qualified and were accepted to participate in the Cobb Educational Foundation for college," he said. (*See letter on pages 71-73.*)

"You have sent me something I have for many months wanted, that is to see the pictures of the boys

Cobb in 1923.

and girls, also their records and what those in their interest for each thought of their qualifications. You have pleased me much."

You could tell just how much the Foundation had become a part of Cobb's life.

"You cannot imagine how much pleasure I derive from reading over these who I feel are so very close to me," he continued. "Also, I have enjoyed showing a few of my very close friends what we are doing and the quality of these boys and girls."

"About all I had were some clippings and cancelled checks as evidence of my desire along these lines as above," Cobb pointed out. "What you have sent me brings me so very close to those that I am trying to help

and hasten to say it's all very close to my heart."

Had Cobb not made similar statements in earlier years to Miss Merchant, one would think that he had never received such information in the past. But, records show that he, in fact, had received information and pictures of previous scholarship recipients...and had made similar remarks. Perhaps he had forgotten or his filing system was not adequate, or perhaps Frances Cobb took the early scrapbooks with her when she divorced him earlier that year (May 1956).

At any rate, it was clear that Cobb was proud of the students. "I feel sure we will have some real successes as men and women and that is all that it's about," he said. "I am enjoying a great thrill and personal satisfaction."

Cobb was "on a roll" in this July 26 letter, just as he often was when he wrote to Dr. Elkin during the first couple of years of the Foundation. Obviously, he had developed a close relationship with Miss McMahon, as the following post script to his letter shows.

"P.S. This naturally is a personal letter to you, also has something to do in this as to your capacity," he wrote, "as you have so much to do in selections [and] the final screening. We like doctors much but we must have a balance. Many in other fields can go high in life and reflect credit toward this Foundation, even if so modest. No college or university should take the "ball" and run with it to guide [students] to any one institution or profession. This Foundation is for [the] benefit of Georgia boys and girls who qualify as to their work and ratings, also needs, and make known their desires to institution etc."

"I think we have a fine organization Board, etc.," he continued in the footnote, "that also means you. I have an unusual regard for Dr. Caldwell with his interest and integrity – TRC."

Then, as was often the case in his letters, he couldn't stop...even after he had stopped. Next came a brief note on how the Foundation should explain to students about the need for obtaining their grades. "We are interested in keeping them striving, this gains success to strive," he said. Checking on the students would "not be a reprimand," he added.

In an August 23, 1956, letter to Ty Cobb, Miss McMahon apologized for the delay in answering Ty's July 26 letter and noted that a few photographs of students still had not been received. Folders would be copied and sent to him when they were complete, she pointed out.

"I have enjoyed working with you, Dr. Elkin, and the others this year," she said before closing. "Of course, no one could praise Mr. Caldwell too highly to me. He is a wonderful person and so sympathetic. We were both interested in the letters that were written in support of the various students who applied for scholarships."

"In a world that seems to be so well off, there certainly is a great amount of need," she concluded.

The file takes another jump with notations and letters missing until early June when Miss McMahon was trying to set up the 1957 annual meeting. Ty Cobb wrote to her in a June 10, 1957, letter from Menlo Park, California, talking about how he received his mail, and about a young man named Selleck who had visited with him in California. (See copy of letter on page 74.)

A week later (on June 17, 1957), Miss McMahon received another 2-pager, asking for copies of letters about specific students and telling her that a date of July 24th suited him for the next meeting. "I can go to Cooperstown July 22nd and plane down for above date," he wrote, "then to Royston for some house plans and back to New York for July 27th." He also talked about meeting with a "nice and personable" girl (a Miss Slaton) from Royston who had been selected as a scholarship recipient the year before, and about another girl (a Miss Winn) who lived close to Royston and would be an applicant. (See copy of letter on page 74.)

The final date for the 1957 annual meeting turned out to be difficult to schedule, due to various travel arrangements of board members. Ty Cobb was in the process of trying to move from Menlo Park, California, to Cornelia, Georgia; Dr. Elkin, who was now retired from Emory and living in Lancaster, Kentucky, could not return during July; Happy Chandler was in the middle of his sec-

ond term as governor of Kentucky and was out of the country until September; and Dr. Kennedy had health and scheduling problems from his Michigan home.

"I am extremely sorry that circumstances make it impossible for me to be with you and send personal greetings to Mr. Cobb, Dr. Caldwell, Dr. Elkin and yourself," Dr. Kennedy wrote in a July 25, 1957, response about applicants to Miss McMahon. "As you know, I have not met Governor Chandler or Mr. Combs, but if they should be on hand please express my greetings to them as well as regrets that I cannot be there to shake them by the hand."

Finally, the board members who could attend met in Atlanta on August 21, 1957. Scholarships totaling $11,900.00 were granted to 29 students (13 renewals and 16 new) for the 1957-58 year. It was a new record for the Foundation, which had started with only six scholarships in 1954-55, followed by 11 in 1955-56, and 23 in 1956-57.

By this time in his life (late 1957), Ty Cobb had become a lonely man by many accounts. He had two homes on the west coast – one in Menlo Park, California, and one in Lake Tahoe, Nevada, but both were in poor condition. Menlo Park and Atherton, where he first moved his family in the 1930s, are small suburbs on the southern edge of the San Francisco peninsula. According to Al Stump in his book, Cobb: A Biography, the California home was an 11-room, two-story, richly landscaped Spanish villa located in an exclusive neighborhood. But, by the late 1950s, the home was run-down and had no lights, no heat, and no hot water. "It was in blackout," Stump wrote, quoting Cobb: "I'm suing the Pacific Gas and Electric Company for overcharging me on the service. Those rinky-dinks tacked an extra 16 dollars on my bill. Bunch of crooks. When I wouldn't pay, they cut off my utilities. Okay – I'll see them in court."

Unhappy with his surroundings, Cobb had decided to move back to Georgia to build a third retirement home. Locating some property near Cornelia, which wasn't too far from Royston, he started working on his plans.

It has been mentioned that Cobb and Taylor Spink, publisher of the Sporting News, had maintained a close friendship and correspondence for several decades. The Sporting News has a web site (www.sportingnews.com/

archives/Ty) with a number of letters posted from Ty Cobb to Spink. One of those letters, dated September 2, 1957, talks about his new home in Georgia.

"Am much pleased by plans here, have an unusual site to build on a mountain just out of this town some 70 acres, rhododendron, dogwood, hemlock, oak and pine dense, have to clear out a lot," Cobb wrote. "I can see my grandfather's place where I was taken to be born some 4 miles down below my house site," he continued, giving a detailed description of how far he would be from various towns.

"I am extremely happy about it all, busy with architect, plans, details, etc.," he said. "Friends and all the people are so fine & helpful to me, but Royston was much disappointed, had trouble about proper site down there also much better there than here. I have more relatives around Cornelia than Royston and will be only 40 minutes to Royston."

An October 7, 1957, letter from Cobb to Miss McMahon was different from any other in the Foundation files – it was typed! Presented on his Menlo Park, California, letterhead, Cobb said he had received the report of new students which "is appreciated very much." *(See copy of letter, plus an insert copy from the Detroit Baseball Company on pages 75-77.)*

Then, he quickly switched gears in the second paragraph. "I have just sent away part of my belongings here by van to Georgia so I am in the process of moving," he wrote. "I have more details to contend with which I am sending to Georgia so I can answer when I am settled there."

"I have a home rented until my real home is completed so I shall try to have a little time to myself in Cornelia to take care of all this. At the present it has been a little too much for me and all I have to do."

Then comes another change in thought. "I am enclosing two checks, which is a donation to the Ty Cobb Educational Fund," he wrote, following that with a feeling that he should not endorse the checks "as they will constitute a receipt from me of these funds and will then have to be accounted for in my income tax."

The note from the Detroit Baseball Company indicated two checks, totaling $2,647.38, represented receipts from the "Ty Cobb Night" in Augusta. "We are very happy to forward these to you for your use in the

Ty Cobb Foundation." One of the checks was for $500.00 and the other for $2,147.38.

A note on Ty Cobb's life should be inserted here. For some or many reasons, the baseball great never built that dream home in Cornelia and spent the last few years of his life traveling back and forth from Georgia to California and other places. Much of this time was spent in hospitals, taking treatments for his many illnesses.

In the book, Ty Cobb, author Charles C. Alexander wrote that Cobb wanted to live on Chenoocetah Mountain near Cornelia to "be by myself while I rest." For a time, he lived with Harrison Gailey, his cousin, before moving into the town's only modern apartment complex. Once settled, he wanted to travel to colleges around the state and meet Cobb Educational Fund scholars.

"But, for all his good intentions, Cobb was an old man and was no better able to relax and remain in one place than he had been as a ballplayer during the off seasons," Alexander wrote. Since July 1957 he had been on the go, crossing and recrossing the country three times, and talking with architects and contractors. He couldn't stay in one place too long.

During the last few years of his life, which coincided with the early years of the Educational Fund, Cobb received money from numerous speeches and appearances and mailed the checks to the Foundation. Such was probably the case from a May 21, 1958, note from Thomas Park at Trust Company acknowledging a check in the amount of $250 from Cobb and his Lake Tahoe home.

In a 4-page note to Ms. McMahon, dated May 6, 1958, Cobb started with "enclosed find a check, please see this reaches proper source." Park's note indicates the check made it into the Fund's banking account.

"I plan returning to Georgia within 10 days and hope to contact Dr. Caldwell and go over some future plans relative to our set up and get his opinion on some matters pertaining to future selections and general procedures per the Educational Foundation," Ty continued in the May 6, 1958, letter, apparently from California.

He noted that he had lost the original Trust document during his back-and-forth moves from California to Georgia, and asked Miss McMahon to locate a copy for him. "I know generally what the set up is but want to review same towards making some permanent plans as to amounts of stock or funds to establish an amount of income to perpetuate a certain expenditure to accommodate a set number of students that we can afford to underwrite in college," he rambled on. (*See copy of note on pages 78.*)

Then, he became more specific in his desires for scholarship recipients. "I would like to ask Dr. Caldwell to give thought to the subject of giving preference to male applicants over the girl applicants," he said. "The girls are smart and they qualify, but they go on and a great percentage lose their identity, marry and lose their name. Also will not follow up in what we want. I hope Dr. Caldwell and you will understand in my crude way of expressing this. I hope to explain my idea better later, [but I] think we should try to influence boys into science channels and with the medicine (doctors) or the law."

"This to try and 'take on' boys that may go on and better reflect credit on our Educational Foundation," he concluded. He added that in their last meeting he sensed that "better judgments thought we should select students only from an accredited school."

Setting up the 1958 meeting of the Board of Trustees started in May with a letter from Dr. Elkin in his Lancaster, Kentucky, home to Dr. Caldwell. "I have been ill and in the hospital or would have written you sooner," Dr. Elkin wrote. "I take it that we should have a meeting of the Cobb Foundation early in July. I have not heard from Ty since Christmas and have no idea as to his activities."

Dr. Caldwell responded in a May 28, 1958, letter to Dr. Elkin. "It has been quite a while since any of us here saw Mr. Ty Cobb. Miss McMahon tells me that he has recently returned from California and that he is now at his home in Cornelia. As soon as we have an opportunity to talk with him, we shall try to agree on some tentative dates for the next meeting of the Trustees of the Cobb Foundation."

Then, in a June 13, 1958, letter to Dr. Elkin, Dr. Caldwell reported that "Neither Miss McMahon nor I have yet heard from Mr. Ty Cobb," but that he had read in the paper that Ty had decided not to settle in Cornelia after all. "I presume that we shall hear from Mr. Cobb soon," he said. "When we have an opportunity to talk to him we shall try to agree on certain tentative dates for the meeting of the Trustees."

A June 21, 1958, note from Dr. Elkin to Dr. Caldwell kept the question alive. "I've heard nothing from Ty – after two letters – He is usually a great letter writer," he said. "It is most important for him to be at the meeting – for obvious reasons, but I fear we will have to have the meeting in July on account of renewals, etc. I will contact Earle Combs here next week."

To which Dr. Caldwell responded on June 23. "I do not understand the reasons for Mr. Cobb's failure to reply to your letters and to Miss McMahon's letters about a date for the next meeting of the Board of Trustees," he wrote. "I agree with you that we should have a meeting in July, but we cannot make any definite awards of scholarships until we have the assurance of Mr. Cobb that additional money will be available."

Cobb with William Jennings Bryan at Navin Field in Detroit, 1924.

Now it was in print: "assurance that ADDITIONAL MONEY would be available!"

Two days later, in a June 25, 1958, note, Miss McMahon notified Trustees that the annual meeting of the board would begin at 10:00 A.M. on Thursday, July 31. But there still was no word from Ty Cobb.

A letter in the file, not dated except for "Saturday," was in line to have been written about this time, possibly in late June or early July. The letter, written on C. N. Weatherly Company letterhead from Royston, revealed that Ty Cobb indeed was back in Royston (or Cornelia). Ty indicated that he was in a "rat race" and loaded down with mail created from an incorrect news release. He had been to Atlanta the week before and dropped in on Dr. Caldwell and Miss McMahon a day earlier than expected, and was attempting to explain the mistake. *(See copy of letter on pages 79-80.)*

In the letter, Cobb wanted Miss McMahon to contact a reporter from *LIFE* magazine and give him the "details of the set up of the Educational Fund which would correct the garbled story by *Herald-Telegram* paper, N.Y."

"I am sorry to load all this upon you but I want to be relieved of having to reply to them," he said. Then, with a usual postscript that wound its way across the bottom of the paper and snaked up the side because of a lack of space, Cobb said he was heading back to Menlo Park, California, for several weeks.

Glove and signed ball that reside in the Ty Cobb Museum.

Dr. Elkin (June 28), Earle Combs (July 1), and Ty Cobb (July 28) all responded to Miss McMahon's notice, each saying they would attend the July 31, 1958, meeting. "I plan on being at meeting July 31st at the set time," Cobb wrote. "Hope will have copy of our Trust set up. I received one but per flood of mail and a short time effort to find it, haven't located." Then, up jumps that filing problem again. "I simply have no filing facilities nor anyone to file so bear with me in my travail," he said. *(See note on page 81.)*

When the meeting was held, and for reasons not clear, final decisions could not be reached. "You will find enclosed a list of 17 applicants that have been chosen from the last list," Miss McMahon wrote to Trustees in an August 2, 1958, letter. "We would appreciate it if you would check 10 or 12 of the names and return the single sheet to us. We will then try to compile a list of the students who receive the most votes and make the final awards."

Earle Combs, who had made the trip from Kentucky, wrote to Miss McMahon, making his selections and apologizing for having to leave the meeting early. "Personally I could see no reason why we couldn't have made the selections while we were all together," he wrote. "It was so nice seeing you again and I assure you it was a pleasure working with you and making these selections. You are to be congratulated for the fine manner in which you handle the whole set up."

Ty Cobb's response was in a Western Union telegram dated August 29, 1958. "My selection numbers one two three four nine ten twelve fourteen fifteen sixteen and seventeen. List for selection follows air mail," the telegram stated.

Cobb's written response was dated a day earlier (August 28, 1958), saying that he was very sorry about being late and that he hoped it would arrive in time.

Then came another pitch for boys. "Think we should give boys preference, also lean towards science," he said. "Have done this very crudely. I have not been well, had a very trying trip out by auto, long distance also <u>very</u> hot." The note was on a Nevada letterhead. "My address will be Menlo Park, California as I am to be there for a few days, then back here (Nevada?) to rest up. But Menlo Park will be forwarded if [I] should not be there." *(See copy of telegram and note on pages 82-83.)*

Foundation files do not tell the whole story, but a July 15, 1958, note from Trust Company listed $3,435.23 in "transfers from income." It included additions to the Fund such as: proceeds from the sale of 200 shares of General Motors Corporation stock, $8,021.09; contributions received as proceeds from "Ty Cobb Night" in Augusta, $2,647.38; contributions received from Union Leader Fund of Manchester, New Hampshire, $500.00; contributions received from United Newspapers Magazine Corporation, $250.00; and credits of unused portions of two grants, $333.34.

Assets on hand prior to the annual meeting of the Foundation that July included: 2,000 shares of AT&T common stock, with a market value $2,222.00; 500

shares of Coca-Cola stock, valued at $58,125.00; 521 units of Common Trust Fund, valued at $8,497.51; 600 shares of General Motors Corporation stock, valued at $24,075.00; and $998.00 in cash.

The grand total in this, only the fifth year of the Ty Cobb Fund, was $93,917.51. Trustees approved 32 scholarships, 12 new and 20 renewals, during that July 31 meeting, providing $12,300.00 funds for the 1958-59 school year. The files do not point out how many of the 17 students (mentioned in Miss McMahon's letter) actually received scholarships.

The final communication in the Foundation files for 1958 was a three-page letter from Ty Cobb to Miss McMahon, dated October 10, 1958.

"First is enclosed a check for Trust Co. to be credited to Educational Fund," he wrote, getting what appeared to be a personal thing off his chest and out of the way at the beginning of the letter.

Then, he went into a paragraph about how much better he was feeling, having developed "a fine system of conditioning" that had eased his tension. "I am on Lake Tahoe with plenty of room away from cities, etc.," he wrote. "Briefly my case is a very (or was) highly developed one of tension."

Next Cobb wanted to know about the students selected in July and that if any of them were on his list. Then he launched into a discussion about a girl applicant from Emmanuel College, "near Royston, GA, my home," noting that she might deserve her high marks, but maybe not in comparison to students from more highly accredited schools. "Because one is from Royston, Georgia area, my home, they should not be shown any preference," he said.

Cobb spent the next paragraph emphasizing that he agreed with Dr. Caldwell about the accreditation issue. And, for the first time in the files, his pen filled with the usual green ink, ran out and he refilled it with brown ink. "Ink refill wrong color," he explained, as if it wasn't obvious.

We're now approaching the end of the second page in his three-page letter before his real reason for writing begins to emerge...except for the opening sentence, that is. His feelings apparently had been somewhat hurt.

"The question of finances were mentioned," he said, obviously referring to the last meeting of the Trustees. "I stated that was my obligation and would surely be taken care of, it was, and for Dr. Caldwell and your

information only, in this year and before 1959, the Educational Foundation with the Trust Co. of Georgia, will have a very appreciable amount of money or stocks at their disposal for future use.

"I do not think my position as donor and my plans of procedure per my desire and wish be questioned," he stressed. "This happens to be my obligation and I do have a deep feeling relative to any obligation or desires that I initiate. I do get a deep sense of happiness in what I am doing."

Then he went into a process of thanking all involved with the Foundation. "I am very deeply appreciative of so much fine unselfishness of those who are connected with this project," he said. (*See copy of letter on pages 84-85.*)

There was no communication in the files about receiving such a check or stock certificate during late 1958.

The files were silent again in early 1959, either by design or happening. But things began to pick up again in May when Miss McMahon received a letter from Dr. Charles Kennedy of Michigan. "I have just had a letter from Mr. Cobb telling me that he has asked that the date for the Cobb Foundation Annual Meeting be held either before or after July 22 and 23, since those appear to be the dates set for a celebration in Cooperstown," Dr. Kennedy wrote. "He has asked me to join him in Cooperstown and to try to work out a schedule with which will be satisfactory to all around."

Then came a May 24, 1959, letter from Ty Cobb. "Enclosed find check for Educational Foundation, first time in my life a recompense for a number of balls to be autographed and returned," he said. "A promotion project in entertaining this company's field organization."

Cobb quickly switched gears. "Dr. Kennedy will write you about arrangement of dates in Atlanta for Educational Fund meeting," he said, noting that the Detroit doctor planned to attend the Foundation meeting, but also had a still-unscheduled meeting with the Regents of the University of Michigan to consider. "I must be in Cooperstown, N.Y. (for the) annual celebration of Baseball's Hall of Fame [on the] 19th, 20th and 21st of July," Cobb said. (*See copy of Cobb's letter on page 85, and a copy of Kennedy's note on page 86.*)

Dr. Kennedy wrote back on May 26, noting again that he had been invited to Cooperstown and that the meeting in Ann Arbor, Michigan, still had not been set.

So, he had decided to set aside the week of July 20-25 for the Cobb Foundation meeting.

It took several more letters between the three parties of Ty Cobb, Dr. Caldwell, and Dr. Kennedy before a meeting was finally set for Thursday, July 16, 1959. Earle Combs, now the commissioner for the Department of Banking in Frankfort, Kentucky, wrote that he could not attend the meeting.

The other Kentuckian, Gov. Chandler, wrote that he had placed the date on his calendar and was "hopeful that my schedule will permit me to be with you."

There was no mention in the files of exactly who attended the meeting, but Trustees awarded a record number of 37 scholarships in the amount of $14,200 for the 1959-60 school year.

The 1959 meeting must have been a sad occasion, for it was the first one held following the death of the Foundation's first Chairman and Ty Cobb's longtime friend, Dr. Daniel C. Elkin. Following a long illness, Dr. Elkin died at his Kentucky home on November 3, 1958.

But, since Dr. Elkin had moved from Atlanta several years before, Dr. Caldwell had taken over most of the duties of the Foundation. With his secretary, Miss McMahon, also handling the secretarial duties, the unofficial office of the Ty Cobb Educational Foundation had already moved to the Board of Regents office.

So now the move became official. Dr. Caldwell was named chairman of the board, and Dr. Merritt B. Hoag, President of North Georgia College, and Dr. H. Prentice (Dean) Miller of Emory University were appointed to the board.

"I think that you and Miss McMahon conducted a very successful meeting for the Cobb Foundation in Atlanta a few days ago," Dr. Kennedy wrote in a July 28 letter to Dr. Caldwell. "The whole affair was very gratifying to me, although, I think you will agree with me that occasionally it was a bit strenuous."

He mentioned that Ty had come to Detroit for three or four days after leaving Cooperstown. "I again assure you that I think you are all doing a wonderful job for the Cobb Fund and I am very sure the appointments made of the new members on the Board will be most helpful," he concluded.

Dr. Caldwell responded: "We are so glad that you were able to attend the meeting of the Trustees of the Cobb Foundation. You made a significant contribution

to the meeting and your presence meant a great deal to Mr. Cobb and to all of us."

In a short note to Miss McMahon on September 28, 1959, Ty Cobb sent another check and noted that he was getting rested up after the trip to Atlanta, Cooperstown, Detroit, and maybe other points not mentioned anywhere. Then, he asked if the Foundation had some students studying for the ministry. (*See copy of note on page 87.*)

In an October 2 reply to Cobb, Miss McMahon identified two scholarship students who were studying for the ministry, providing information about both boys. "I think these are the only two we have studying for the ministry," she said.

Cobb answered back on October 12, 1959, feeling the need to explain his request. "No doubt you wondered my request and I must, I feel, explain," he wrote, "and you can tell Dr. Caldwell but no one else as I do not seek credit."

Then he explained. Cobb had cashed a check for someone and then lost it. Asking for a replacement, he was told "it's your hard luck and your loss." Cobb said he prayed a selfish prayer to God, revealing the wrongs of this person and promising "if I received this small amount due me, that I would use it in some way for God's work."

Well, he finally got the check replaced, cashed it, and sent $100 each to the two students. "These two boys in Divinity schools are receiving now in the mail one hundred dollars each, extra to what we are giving them," he said. "I am allowed a real happiness in this act. I think this way is so very right." (*See copy of letter on pages 88-89.*)

As sort of a post script to the letter, Cobb changed gears: "Trust Co. has a very sizable amount as surplus, now." Records indicate that the "surplus" was reaching or had passed the $100,000 mark by September 1959. (*Just over a year later, on December 31, 1960, the total would jump to $144,030.00.*)

Another change took place in the Foundation's Board of Trustees, sometime late in 1959 or early in 1960. Gov. A. B. "Happy" Chandler, the former Commissioner of Baseball who was nearing the completion of his second term as governor of Kentucky, resigned from the board. There was no official documentation of the resignation, but Gov. Chandler had never really been an active member.

Ty Cobb was busy making speeches and making money for his Educational Foundation during this period of his life, even though he must have known his time on earth was drawing to a close. In September, he had experienced problems while on a hunting expedition and was hardly able to walk. Frances Cass, his second wife who had changed her name from Cobb following her divorce, heard of his illness and went to him in his Lake Tahoe lodge. Eventually, she managed to convince Cobb to enter the Scripps Clinic in La Jolla, California, for a physical examination.

There *(as also reported in another chapter of this publication)* the doctors found that Cobb had diabetes; a weak heart; high blood pressure; an enlarged prostate gland; and Bright's disease, a degenerative kidney condition. Fighting the diseases with medications and bourbon, Cobb became dissatisfied with the doctors' decisions in early December 1959 and headed to Emory University in Atlanta for an examination by a medical staff he knew fairly well and was inclined to trust.

At Emory, he found that he didn't have Bright's dis-ease after all, but rather an enlarged prostate with a cancerous growth that had spread rapidly to other parts of the body. Following surgery and cobalt radiation treatments he returned to the west coast to continue his struggles with the state of California.

On December 5, 1959, Cobb wrote a short note to Miss McMahon, but didn't mention his illnesses. "Another check for [the] Educational Foundation," he wrote. "I will or should be in Atlanta before you receive this. I shall call Dr. Caldwell when I get settled there for a few days. Leaving here tonight shortly after midnight." *(See copy of note on page 90.)*

A longer note, dated January 17, 1960, on stationery from Cobb Memorial Hospital, enclosed yet another check, this one for $500. "Enclosed find check for our Educational Foundation," he said, asking Miss McMahon to make formal acknowledgment to Max Kase, chairman of a memorial dinner sponsored by Sports Lodge, B'nai B'rith in New York City. *(See copy of letter on pages 91-92.)*

Unlike previous communications, this one was written front and back on the Hospital letterhead. "Might see Dr. Caldwell and yourself some day of the coming week," he

Ted Williams and Cobb in 1961, the last year of Cobb's life.

said, before ending with a usual P.S. about a "real prospect" for the following year's scholarship program.

Then he concluded with his first mention of illness. "Am not a patient here, rest and proper schedule carrying out process, close to Emory doctors, also New York where I have to go January 24th and 31st, then back to Emory for final decisions, etc."

Another one-page note, dated March 2, 1960, arrived on a Menlo Park, California, letterhead. "Here is a small check," he started. "You might acknowledge this with expressions of appreciation, this is a Jewish check." This one was for $250 from B'nai B'rith, Boston

Cobb shows his jovial spirit.

Sports Lodge in Boston, Massachusetts.

Then, he talked briefly about his health. "I am feeling fairly well, sorry I missed seeing you. I appreciate very much your thought in calling."

Ending with a usual P.S., Cobb noted that a Miss Templeton had visited with him. "She is a student at Emory, a very impressive fine little girl," he said. "I would say we are complemented to have her."

In a second postscript he noted that Jimmy Butts had called on him a second time. "He is very popular and scoring very well." (*See copy of note on page 93.*)

Cobb obviously was feeling better a few months later, as a seven-page-plus letter dated May 26, 1960, arrived from Menlo Park, California. He was answering a May 16 letter from Miss McMahon, and launched heavily into a number of subjects. (*See copy of letter on pages 94-98.*)

Once again, Cobb placed an emphasis on "applicants" sending photos along with their applications. "This is a <u>must</u> and would like you to stress this in future, no photo, no consideration," he said, following with his reasons. "Let's stress this and bring all brochures up to date."

Cobb then switched to his hospital stay at Emory and to a scholarship recipient who visited him there. "I had never seen her, she lives in Blythe, Georgia, close to Augusta," he wrote. "We had chosen her, she was one of ours, there she presented herself and to my judgment about the finest little gal I have seen. She seems to really have all it takes, a perfect little person as a female, wide eyes, a fine little lady, serious, wish she was my daughter, though mine are really tops."

Still rambling, Cobb switched back to the photo issue, indicating that he would have known this girl, a Miss Templeton, if he had seen her photo (not knowing, of course, whether or not there was a photo on file). "It would help a lot for all to show pictures in our decision to accept them," he said.

Then he went into another reason for photos, noting that "if the crop [of applicants] should not be so good, we are not wedded to any number to accept" and would be able to eliminate some by their photos. He also added that the number of scholarships is not fixed, "but I am sort of fixing 36 in number of boys and girls that I can continue to help." He said that he was working with Mr. Parks at Trust Company Bank and "I now know close to the amount of money or securities" that would be needed to endow "this Educational Foundation to carry on in perpetuity. This will be done within this year."

He then switched to building his 5-room house in Cornelia and that he was donating his house in California to the Educational Foundation "to eliminate a considerable capital gains tax."

Switching again, he talked of when he could be in Atlanta for the Foundation's annual meeting, working it around another trip to Cooperstown and the Hall of Fame's annual meeting, an annual meeting with trustees at the Royston Memorial Hospital, and a trip to attend the Olympics in Rome during late August and early September, then back to this country to attend the World Series in October.

Then, he switched to health issues. "I am not well, also not really sick," he said. "After my operation there in Emory I was placed on a line of medication, I would term it a cleansing, and trying to eliminate the causes of my operation which relieved me much. These medicines is [sic] what causes me now a much underpar feeling. I am 'wailing' about, so not too serious, [but at] my age of 73, [I] am or have not in all my life been used to the underpar feelings. I hope I am making all this understandable."

By now, he was at the end of his fifth page in this hand-written (green ink as usual) letter. He followed this with two more pages, the last one of which, he wrote all around the four edges of the paper, trying to get in what he thought would be his final "P.S." which followed each letter. He ran out of space, however, and had to finish on the back of the page, something he rarely ever did in his writings.

In those last two pages, Cobb wrote about a number of scholarship students that he was following, including Jimmy Butts, an original recipient who would be graduating, and Miss Templeton (mentioned earlier in this letter) who visited him at Emory. Then came this one: "Our star as of now is Jerry Sutton of Johns Hopkins," he said, noting that "they are now offering him a professorship when he graduates."

"These matters thrill me, Miss McMahon and Dr. Caldwell," he continued. "I hope we can take care of him even more substantially in our next meeting."

Cobb then apologized for the lengthy letter. "Long letters are not in proper form," he wrote. "I am sorry for the infliction, but even so, I enjoy the labor of writing all this. Yes, we have others (referring to scholarship recipients) but cannot cope with all of each of our boys and girls."

In his first "P.S." Cobb mentioned yet another student. Around the edges of the page he talked about moving to Nevada, and that the Foundation stationery should be changed to leave off Happy Chandler and to put on "Miller and the other man, and bring all this up to date." He also suggested adding Elkin and Rankin as deceased members of the board, and then on the back of the page, apologized yet again.

"I have, after finishing this jumbled letter, [realized] that you have thought of [these changes] and have the proper change of stationery heading," he concluded.

Things changed quickly for Ty Cobb at this stage in his life, as a June 14, 1960, letter indicates. Following that long letter in late May, Cobb wrote a short two-pager on small Nevada stationery. Noting that Miss McMahon had indicated a meeting of the board in early June, Cobb wrote that "it would suit me perfectly" and that he could "leave here any time now for this meeting."

Cobb mentioned again, as he had in the May letter, that he "must" attend a meeting at Cobb Memorial Hospital in Royston, the Educational Foundation meeting in Atlanta, and the Hall of Fame meeting in Cooperstown, New York. (See copy of letter on pages 99-100.)

Helping to set the date for the 1960 meeting of the board was significant – it would be his last with the Foundation, for in 1961, he would be suffering through the last days of his life at Emory Hospital.

The Ty Cobb files do not tell us who attended the 1960 meeting of the Board of Trustees or the exact date when it was convened. We do know, however, that 37 scholarships were awarded for the 1960-61 academic year, 25 new and 12 renewals, for a total of $15,300. Junior college students received $300, senior college students were awarded $400 and professionals received $500 each.

Cobb likely attended the meeting in Atlanta, as well as the Cobb Memorial Hospital meeting in Royston and the Hall of Fame meeting in Cooperstown, New York. It is documented in a number of books that he actually flew to Rome for the Olympic games and was back in this country for the World Series.

The 1960 annual meeting would have been the second for Dr. Caldwell as board chairman. If Cobb attended, he likely met for the last time with Dr. Caldwell, Dr. Miller, and Dr. Hoag. Gov. Chandler of Kentucky had resigned the year before and, of course, did not attend. Mr. Combs of Kentucky had new responsibilities that would force him to resign later in the year. And, an August 5, 1960, letter in the files from Dr. Kennedy indicates (although not saying so) that he had not attended.

"It was good to have your wonderful report and fine

to learn about the excellent records being made in upwards of thirty different colleges," Dr. Kennedy wrote to Miss McMahon.

"I also note that the girls are still a goodly number," he continued. "Mr. Cobb has apparently changed his mind on that one a bit since last year and maybe some of my conversation was helpful," he said, referring to the expressions of Ty Cobb that the Foundation should favor boys, especially in science.

Only four days after Dr. Kennedy's letter came an August 9, 1960, letter from Earle Combs, noting that he had accepted a new position with his insurance company and could not give the Cobb Foundation "the time that a Trustee should give."

In tendering his resignation, Combs, who would be voted into baseball's Hall of Fame later in his life, said: "I am also of the opinion that inasmuch as the Cobb Foundation is for Georgia Students that the Trustees should be composed of Georgia men as they, in my opinion, would be in a better position to pass on each student."

Ty Cobb returned to his writing trail to Miss McMahon with a November 5, 1960, letter detailing a number of subjects. *(See letter and note on page 101.)*

For one, it seems that his "very fine young lady" named Miss Templeton was no longer in his favor. It seems that Miss Theresa Gailey, daughter of his cousin, Harrison Gailey of Royston, was accepted at Emory University and Ty wanted her to meet with Miss Templeton. When he couldn't find her, he wrote to her home in Blythe, Georgia, asking that the letter be forwarded. Eventually he received a wedding invitation from Miss Templeton, "I believe Nashville, Tennessee," he said in his letter. "I in no way think or believe Miss Templeton has not reported this to you, so she could be eliminated from our sponsorship. Please advise me of this."

Then, as customary, he quickly changed gears, noting that he was not "real happy from a physical standpoint" even though he did "take off from hospital out here for Olympic Games." He said that his hospital visit "was for mechanical treatments," a series that he would have to keep up at intervals. "Hence the liberty of trip to Rome, Etc.," he said.

Switching gears yet again, he told of how busy he was at his Lake Tahoe, Nevada, home working on his book, and that he was happy that he did not "drag" Dr. Caldwell into this "time, and mass of work, research, Etc., rehashing, polishing up, meeting with publishers." He noted that he would have written to Dr. Caldwell about this, but "he, I feel, is too busy coping with my letters, Etc."

Then he talked about the weather in Lake Tahoe and that he soon would be leaving by auto to Georgia. "I have some plans there that I must meet and carry out," he said, noting that after the Georgia trip he would travel to Phoenix, Arizona, "for that fine and mild climate."

In the first of three "P.S." additions, Cobb talked again of hearing from Jerry Sutton at Johns Hopkins.

The second addition included his request that if any recipients be warned if they "slow up and rest too much on their oars and hold our keep cheaply." And, if they fail to "heed and marks sag" at the end of the year "let's drop them."

A final note was attached to the three-page letter, explaining that "my stay in Georgia will be to carry out the endowment of Cobb Educational Foundation."

As part of a November 21, 1960, letter to Ty Cobb, Dr. Caldwell wrote: "Miss McMahon let me read a letter that she received from you several days ago. I was glad to learn about some of the activities in which you are now engaged. I hope that the work on your biography is not proving too burdensome. And I sincerely hope and pray that your physical condition is getting better."

Cobb's next letter in the files was a short one, written from Cornelia, Georgia, on February 25, 1961. The note, which Cobb had marked through Glenbrook, Douglas County, Nevada, and written in Cornelia, was cut off and did not include Cobb's signature.

"Your letter received relative to Jack Colwell and I certainly concur with your idea of dropping him," Cobb wrote, obviously referring to a student that Miss McMahon had written to him about.

"He sounds like a first class 'learner'," Cobb continued. "The first paragraph of his letter per reinstatement lines doesn't ring so good." *(See copy of letter on pages 102-103.)*

Later in the note Cobb said that "I do not like to interfere in any way any decisions or actions of the Foundation." But, in reality, he actually did!

Then he switched to his health. "I am doing as well

as should expect. [I] will say [that] I am not exactly enjoying your Georgia weather."

He concluded his note with travel plans, saying that he would be leaving around March 1 for a stay at the Safari Hotel in Phoenix, Arizona, "for a month or more" before going to Menlo Park, California, and then back to Georgia.

Cobb signed the note in the usual way: "With Kindest regards, I am," and the rest was cut off.

The final letter located in the Ty Cobb Educational Foundation files from Ty Cobb was written on his Nevada stationery, using a blue ink pen.

Written on April 20, 1961, it started in the usual way: "Dear Miss McMahon:-"

"The enclosed is self explanatory," he started. "[I] don't think she will have to be accorded my special consideration, but to be sure, I would like her [to] receive same, if her marks etc. merit it." There is no explanation clarifying this statement about this student.

"Am out here attending some matters and expect to return to Georgia (Cornelia) for quite a stay," he offered in the next paragraph.

"This Loudermilk boy (Cornelia) is another one I wish to be accepted if his marks warrant," Cobb continued. "Need not investigate family financial position. I know them well, fine mother and father, lots of adversity."

The always charitable Cobb and a young boy.

In his first "P.S." Cobb asked Miss McMahon to notify Dr. Kennedy in Michigan "and of course the other members of the board" to attend the next meeting of the Trustees. "A must," he said, double underlining both words. "I have some director medallions to present. T.R.C."

Then, as a usual afterthought, he wrote: "Merely state it is my particular desire all directors be there this particular time." (*See copy of letter on page 104.*)

From his continuous pain, plus the many visits with doctors, Cobb obviously knew his time on earth was drawing to a close.

He entered Emory Hospital for the last time on June 5, 1961, taking with him, according to Al Stump in his book Cobb: A Biography, a brown paper bagful of stocks, bonds and other securities worth some $1 million. He placed the brown bag on a bedside table and atop that placed his Luger pistol. The black gun made his nurses nervous, Stump wrote, and his doctor persuaded him to store the documents in a hospital safe.

Dr. Charles Kennedy of Detroit was in Atlanta to attend the July 14 meeting of the Board of Trustees. He then visited with Cobb "for 10 or 15 minutes during his last lucid interval" on Saturday afternoon, July 15.

Dr. Kennedy rushed downstairs to advise Mrs. Cobb and her family "to hurry to see him while he was still clear." Then he wrote: "It is my understanding that they all visited with him for a short time before he lapsed once more into irrationality from which he never again recovered."

Apparently, no one was with Cobb when he died at 1:20 p.m. on Monday, July 17, 1961. He was five months short of reaching the age of 74.

Cobb had died only three days after the Scholarship Board awarded a record number of 46 scholarships for the 1961-62 year. Included were 21 new awards and 25 renewals, providing $19,000.00 in scholarship funds for Georgia students. The total funds also were a record for the fledging Foundation, starting its eighth year on the scene.

Six months before Cobb's death (December 31, 1960), the market value of the Educational Foundation was at an all-time high of $144,030.00. The Fund had steadily grown from Cobb's original investment of just over $27,312.50 in 1953, having reached $94,356.00 in 1957, and probably advancing above the $100,000.00 level sometime during the 1959-60 academic year (*records aren't clear*).

Trustees obviously knew at the time of the July 1961

meeting that Ty Cobb's life was growing short, and that his death would provide a considerable amount of revenue for the Foundation. Of course, they didn't know exactly how much money, for few people, if indeed anyone, knew how much Cobb was worth.

When Ty Cobb died, his final will and testament provided that 25 percent of his residue and property go to the Ty Cobb Educational Fund, with the remaining 75 percent going to his children and grandchildren. Now, the Educational Fund would be in a position to really make some awards, but, because of his various holdings in stocks, property (in Georgia, Nevada, California and elsewhere) and cash, determining his worth and the amount to be distributed would be no easy task.

Trust Company of Georgia was Cobb's choice as executor of the estate, and, because of the various holdings – plus a civil suit filed by one of his daughters – it took several years to complete the transactions.

Still, on October 19, 1961, Thomas B. Park, the assistant trust officer at Trust Company Bank, wrote to the Educational Fund's Board of Trustees:

"Enclosed is a copy of a letter, dated October 18, 1961, which Mr. Carroll Payne Jones has written to the beneficiaries of the estate of Tyrus R. Cobb," Park wrote. "Attached to the letter is a copy of the original inventory of Mr. Cobb's estate and three sheets on which he has attempted to estimate the status of the estate."

"You will note that he estimates that the amount which the Ty Cobb Educational Fund will receive will be approximately $800,000.00," he concluded. Cobb's estate was then estimated to be about 5.4 million dollars.

Many accounts of Cobb's worth had the baseball great holding as much as $10 to $11 million, which would have provided the Educational Fund with $2.5 million or more. His actual worth, however, probably has never officially been established.

There were some questions about the royalties from Cobb's book, whether they would go directly to the Educational Fund or into the estate. But, since there was no evidence that Cobb actually wanted these royalties to go into the Educational Fund, it was determined that the estate would receive book proceeds. The book,

Ty Cobb and Tris Speaker.

incidentally, did not go into print until after Cobb's death in 1961.

Simply named <u>My Life in Baseball: The True Record</u>, the book was co-authored by Al Stump, a sports writer who spent long stretches of time living with the baseball legend. An autobiography commissioned by Cobb himself, it sold moderately well and was considered by many people as one of the finest books of its kind.

Although it didn't go into print until after Cobb's death, the baseball great had final say over its contents as accorded him by the publisher.

But, Stump didn't stop with this book, following it with an account of his own, simply named <u>Cobb: A Biography</u>. This book was the basis of a movie based on the relationship between Cobb and Stump which was released in late 1994.

In <u>Cobb: A Biography</u>, Stump reported that Ty had been good at analyzing the Dow-Jones averages and playing the stock market. "Twice a week he phoned experts around the country, determined good buys, and bought in blocks of five hundred to fifteen hundred shares," Stump said. "He made money consistently, even when bedridden, with a mind that read behind the fluctuations of a dozen different issues."

"The state of Georgia," he reported Ty as saying, "will realize about a million dollars from inheritance taxes when I'm dead. But there isn't a man alive who knows what I'm worth."

According to the *Sporting News*, as reported in Stump's book, there was evidence upon Cobb's death that his worth approximated $12 million.

An August 1987 issue of *Georgia Trend* magazine reported that Cobb owned about $10 million in General Motors stock and $1.7 million in Coca-Cola stock when he died in 1961.

"Cobb's good timing and shrewdness extended beyond the baseball diamond," writer Leonard Ray Teel said in the Georgia Trend feature entitled "Past Business." He noted that when Cobb was only 20 and fast becoming Georgia's most famous baseball player, that he had capitalized on his success of winning the first of his 12 batting titles in 1907.

"Cobb supplemented his $2,400 salary by signing a contract to endorse Coca-Cola," Teel wrote, adding that a poster pictured him at bat and quoting him saying that between games of a double-header a Coke "refreshes me to such an extent that I can start the sec-

ond game, feeling as if I had not been exercising at all."

Cobb did not fit the turn-of-the-century stereotype of the poor, dumb athlete. "Right from the break-in season," he explained in his autobiography, "I was determined to put myself in a powerful bargaining position. How? Simply by earning some important money on the outside."

Teel reported that Cobb sought reliable insider information that led to solid investments, making him the richest ballplayer of his time. During the early years of car making in Detroit, Cobb found "all the rising tycoons of the newborn auto industry did their drinking and dealing" in the bar of the old Ponchartrain Hotel. Cobb joined the business conversations and soon was invited to become an investor in the fledging industry by Louis Chevrolet, who was joining the competition against Henry Ford's Model T.

In 1907 Cobb bought 50 shares of United Motors, which was later acquired by General Motors. That investment alone became the basis of Cobb's first fortune.

The second fortune grew out of his association with Coca-Cola, Teel wrote. "In 1918, as Cobb told it, the Tigers were in New York to play the Yankees when Cobb saw the young Robert W. Woodruff, who was there raising money to buy the soft drink company from Asa Chandler." They talked for hours one rainy afternoon as Woodruff tried to persuade Cobb to become an investor.

Cobb eventually bought 300 shares of Coke and later increased his holdings to 20,000 shares.

After his retirement from baseball in 1928, Teel wrote that Cobb's two passions became golf and business. "Insider advice helped him ride out the 1929 crash," Teel wrote. "Instead of selling his stock, he bought more shares of Coca-Cola and General Motors, which paid off steadily through the Great Depression. He was an obsessive investor, always studying the stock market averages and traveling with his business papers stuffed in a brown paper sack.

Cobb thrived on the competitiveness of business, Teel wrote. "Away from baseball, I had a lot of fun," Cobb said, "and much of it came in putting myself against the odds found in the financial world, which are somewhat longer against success than getting a base hit."

It would be extremely difficult to determine exactly how much the Educational Fund received from Ty

Cobb's estate. The files of the Foundation provide a paper trail that was long and wide. For example:

– On November 27, 1961, the Fund received 125 shares of Coca-Cola common stock (market value $13,093.75) and $6,906.25 in cash;

– On December 17, 1962, the Fund received 200 shares of Coca-Cola common stock (valued at $17,000.00) and $5,500.00 in cash;

– On December 31, 1960, Trust Company reported the Educational Fund's market value had reached $218,327;

– On July 19, 1963, the Fund received 250 shares of Armco Steel Corporation common stock, valued at $13,687.50;

– On December 9, 1963, the Fund received 125 shares of General Motors common stock (valued at $9,757.82) and $1,500.00 in cash;

– On July 15, 1964, the Fund received $12,500.00 from a cash income from the estate, representing half of the estimated annual income for the year;

– On October 8, 1964, the Fund received $92,041.67 from the sale of Lake Tahoe property, located in Douglas County, Nevada, and the sale of 1,924 shares of Coca-Cola common stock;

– On September 26, 1968, the Fund received $21,804.36 in cash from sales of stock certificates;

– On November 22, 1968, the Fund received $44,219.22, representing principal and interest in connection with a tax settlement with the Treasury Department;

– On December 10, 1968, the Fund received $6,617.09, representing its share from the Georgia estate tax refund.

To make matters worse, two key figures were sidelined late in the process. Furman Smith, Cobb's attorney from the law firm of King & Spalding, died in July 1968, and Tom Park of Trust Company of Georgia suffered a heart attack in September 1968. But, the groundwork had been in place for some time, and the process continued without a hitch.

Another source of income, although probably small in total, came late in 1961 when contributions were made to the Educational Fund from friends of the departed "Georgia Peach." Included was a $1,000.00 gift from R. W. Woodruff of Coca-Cola and a $500.00 contribution from Thomas A. Yawkey, representing the family who owned the Detroit Tigers.

On July 24, 1964, with many of the above exchanges yet to be made, Trust Company provided a list of contributions made to the Educational Fund. At this stage of the settlements, the Bank reported that Cobb had given assets valued at $185,353.06 and "Ty Cobb estate assets" valued at $64,619.28. Thus, the total contributions from Ty Cobb and the Ty Cobb estate were listed at $249,972.34, and additional gifts to the Fund ran the total to $258,504.72.

These "additional gifts" included the proceeds from "Ty Cobb Night" in Augusta, as well as all of the other gifts mentioned above.

Now, the Foundation was ready to take off. Trust Company reported a market value worth at $1,535,069.00 on December 31, 1965. It isn't quite clear when all the funds from the estate were deposited into the Educational Fund (1963-64 records aren't included in the files), but the Fund continued to increase steadily throughout the late 1960s.

Ty Cobb pictured his scholarship fund as providing "maybe 35" scholarships a year. As mentioned in the *Introduction* of this publication, he never in his wildest dreams would have predicted his Ty Cobb Educational Foundation would provide almost $10 million for more than 6,800 Georgia students...nor that his Foundation would be worth more than $15 million (June 31, 1998) in its first 50 years.

But, the facts are there.

The charts on pages 82-83 show the number of scholarships, the amount awarded and the market value of the Foundation through the years. It should be noted here that market value quotations change from hour to hour, day to day, depending upon the stock market. Many of the figures posted on the two pages were values as of June 31 and others as of December 31 of the particular year.

Thus, the highest value ever, and the lowest value, would be difficult to determine.

It's interesting to note that 46 scholarships (and $19,000.00) were awarded in 1961, shortly after Cobb died, and that 67 scholarships (worth $27,133.00) were provided for Georgia students the following year as the Fund increased. The numbers didn't change too drastically during the next few years until 1972 when awards jumped from a record high of 98 in 1971 to a new record high of 150.

Trustees increased it to 180 in 1973 before dropping back a few years. The number of scholarships increased to 193 in 1981, 253 in 1982, and 269 in 1983. Fluctuations in the stock market and increases in the amount of scholarships created various changes in the number of awards through the years.

For example, back in 1960-61 when Cobb was still alive, junior college students received $300 awards, senior college students received $400 awards, and professional students received $500 awards.

During the 1965-66 year, when the Foundation was worth just over $1.5 million, awards were increased to $500 for junior college students, $600 for senior college students, and $700 for professionals. During that year, 61 awards were made – 10 fewer than the year before – for a total of $36,600.00 – $7,134.00 more than the year before.

For the 1969-70 academic year, Trustees increased the awards to $700 for junior college students, $800 for senior college students, and $900 for professionals. During that year, 77 awards were made (21 more than the year before) for a total of $60,766.00, an increase of $22,233 over the year before. And, the market value of the Foundation was at an all-time high of almost $2.4 million.

Awards were increased again in 1972, going to $800 for junior college, $900 for senior college and $1,000 for professionals. In that significant year, Trustees funded 150 scholarships for $135,600.00, record numbers in both categories. And, the market value of the fund had soared above the $3.7 million mark.

More changes in awards followed through the years until reaching $2,000 for both junior college and senior college students, and $3,000 for professionals for the 1988-89 year. With this change, 139 scholarships were awarded for $231,501.00 and the Foundation's worth stood at $4.8 million.

Awards were unchanged for the remaining years in the 50-year history of the Foundation, but scholarship numbers, the total awarded, and the market value have continued to fluctuate as the charts show. Through the first 50 years, the highest number of students receiving scholarships (274), and the record amount of funds distributed ($644,334.00) took place during the 2001-02 academic year.

The market value of the Foundation, as reported by

Trust Company Bank, almost reached the $10 million level in mid-1995 when the figure stood at $9,945,989.00, and it passed the mark the following year at $11,450,138.00. As it closed out its first 50 years, the Foundation's worth was $12,292,406.00. Totals had been higher prior to the June, 2003 figure, but Trustees continued to support a program of over a half million dollars for more than 200 scholarship winners each year.

Cobb in his later career years.

As the Foundation celebrated its 50th anniversary before the start of the 2003-04 academic year, 221 scholarships were awarded in the amount of $528,000.00. That brought the grand total for 50 years to 6,876 awards for $9,743,123.00.

Perhaps "The Georgia Peach" was not a well-liked man in his lifetime, but his dream of "doing something along educational lines" has provided many a smile on the faces of numerous Georgia students down through the years.

And the beat goes on!

HISTORY OF THE TY COBB FUND THROUGH ITS FIRST 50 YEARS

(Market value quotations were posted at different times during the years. Thus, the value of the Foundation has been higher and lower than the posted figures during each year, depending upon the stock market at the time of quotations.

SCHOOL YEAR	SCHOLAR-SHIPS AWARDED	DOLLAR AMOUNT AWARDED	MARKET VALUE OF FOUNDATION	SCHOOL YEAR	SCHOLAR-SHIPS AWARDED	DOLLAR AMOUNT AWARDED	MARKET VALUE OF FOUNDATION
1953-54	0	$ 0.00	$ 27,312.50	1979-80	159	$145,973.00	$ 2,505,653.00
1954-55	6	$ 2,800.00	$ 27,982.07	1980-81	171	$163,200.00	$ 2,303,224.00
1955-56	11	$ 5,500.00	$ 63,127.00	1981-82	193	$185,732.00	$ 2,460,202.00
1956-57	23	$ 8,900.00		1982-83	253	$190,925.00	$ 2,275,118.00
1957-58	29	$ 11,900.00	$ 94,365.00	1983-84	269	$173,562.00	$ 3,007,466.00
1958-59	32	$ 12,300.00	$ 93,917.51	1984-85	215	$179,234.00	$ 2,999,763.00
1959-60	37	$ 14,200.00		1985-86	219	$229,866.00	$ 3,668,479.00
1960-61	37	$ 15,300.00	$ 144,030.00	1986-87	239	$242,165.00	$ 4,835,789.00
1961-62	46	$ 19,000.00		1987-88	166	$173,534.00	$ 5,235,229.00
1962-63	67	$ 27,133.00	$ 218,327.00	1988-89	139	$231,501.00	$ 4,828,343.00
1963-64	72	$ 29,431.00		1989-90	146	$284,802.00	$ 5,778,331.00
1964-65	71	$ 29,466.00		1990-91	124	$280,802.00	$ 6,625,774.00
1965-66	61	$ 36,600.00	$ 1,535,069.00	1991-92	124	$290,004.00	$ 6,989,022.00
1966-67	64	$ 38,050.00	$ 1,508,951.00	1992-93	112	$263,334.00	$ 8,060,162.00
1967-68	65	$ 39,100.00	$ 2,169,727.00	1993-94	97	$228,334.00	$ 8,623,131.00
1968-69	56	$ 38,533.00	$ 2,387,141.00	1994-95	89	$215,002.00	$ 8,203,727.00
1969-70	77	$ 60,766.00	$ 2,397,100.00	1995-96	125	$275,347.00	$ 9,945,989.00
1970-71	80	$ 64,099.00	$ 2,489,626.00	1996-97	204	$457,001.00	$11,450,138.00
1971-72	98	$ 75,828.00	$ 3,027,078.00	1997-98	231	$525,668.00	$13,742,577.00
1972-73	150	$135,600.00	$ 3,729,745.00	1998-99	250	$574,668.00	$15,062,232.00
1973-74	180	$155,300.00	$ 3,355,642.00	1999-00	264	$623,000.00	$15,207,104.00
1974-75	170	$123,500.00	$ 1,961,009.00	2000-01	262	$631,000.00	$14,657,076.00
1975-76	164	$119,015.00	$ 2,531,514.00	2001-02	274	$644,334.00	$13,005,737.00
1976-77	172	$123,181.00	$ 2,548,460.00	2002-03	239	$561,000.00	$13,019,248.00
1977-78	164	$128,633.00	$ 2,505,328.00	2003-04	221	$528,000.00	$12,292,406.00
1978-79	159	$131,000.00	$ 2,616,633.00	**50 Years**	**6,876**	**$9,743,123.00**	

TYRUS R. COBB
GLENBROOK
DOUGLAS COUNTY, NEVADA   8/21/54

Dear "Doc":-

Yours received to day and
we are entertaining some "Kids" here
with ice cream Etc. Tomorrow and
Mrs. Coble has gone for ice so will
snatch this time to write you.
I like your idea of "Hap" I like
him also should there be any
unforseen or thoughtful reason he
could not accept and really "Doc"
I had not thought of any other
course since you were here and
only since I started this letter did
I have the thought I am submitting
should "Happy" have some reason and
I am sure he wont, then lets
think of "Bob" Jones and Senator
George who I know very well.
Really "Doc" when I suffer travail
and many times so unfairly, the
hospital thing and the Educational
thing, helps me much - being a
Doctor you might know without my

57

telling you, that I am very prone
to depressionist feelings, whether
its the years of terrific exertions
and a consequent fibrilating heart
or whether its handed down by
the blood in my veins from
the two sides — I do not know — I
try hard not to inflict my dark
moments upon others, some ten
or 12 years ago, after many years,
infact all my life, I was not
a drinker of alcoholic distillations,
I had many hammer blows in last
12 years, Frances has helped
me wonderfully, I have not damaged
myself, I was not under influence
of alcohol when I was so
ruthlessly treated in the town of
Placerville, this place has a record,
I had a lawyer and they have the
same lineup the Justice of Peace
has a lot of local boys who he
has let loose and treated very
lightly and these boys he selects
as his jury, should anyone
feel outraged and demand a
jury trial — my lawyer told

me also I had, had a previous experience and he told me the same except the former J. P. who was a confirmed alcoholic and fell off a two story porch and was killed, I this time thought the deal was different and employed a lawyer etc. he told me the same story. "Doc" should you ever come this way by auto remember Placerville Calif. dont go through there.

My last lawyer, this time, told me they had made a haul in $300 bonds + fines they got 3 different boys in the air corps from Maxwell Field, Sacramento and up to date for week ends they collected the same as they did from me, you knew "Doc" while I was sorry for these boys My attorney telling me someone else had suffered the same mistreatment really eased my pain now what phycologically could you categary that, my feeling better etc.

Taylor Spinks are coming out for a visit very soon, both are very nice and we tried hard to have them here when "you all" were here. Frances said she wrote Mrs. Elkin a thank you note for the Crownay fish platter (and yes we like it much and its very appropriate.) about the 16th of August she might not have air mailed as she ordinarily would or its possible she did and it was delayed, from your letter posted Aug 19th indicates some delay of same sort.

I enclose prints + negatives of what Frances took with her brag (little) camera, she states they blow up or enlarge wonderfully we would do this but we dont know what size you might want so we send as is, to me, I dont know if you are Crownay Elkin or Crownay Sherlock Holmes with that sporting cap you had on.

Now Frances has some other she took with colored film and when she uses up rest of roll + develop we will send.

I have a very nice letter from Butts, Blairsville, Ga. which am enclosing as he makes certain avowals and am feeling sure he will not have to be prompted by the Trustees, I send it to you and ask you return it so I can enjoy it more later, am sure the selection of this boy was such that he will go through swell.

I did not tell you aunt Nora who sooner or later you will meet and she is quite a person mentally - this boys mother, came for Aunt Nora and she went to Blairsville etc. visit + conversation lasted & lasted some time, Aunt Nora proper, finally had to ask about the boy as I had told her of him because he was from up in My Cobb peoples section, Cobbs N.C. close to Murphy - finally aunt Nora already knowing, if Butts asked his mother where he was, well

she was told the boy was working in the field, of course he must have known aunt Nora was coming there, but he busied himself with the work to be done, I think that is great.

I have a request, could you or secretary contact each of the selected students and ask if I could have a picture of them, no matter the size I can have it blown up, I would like to keep an album, as I enjoy sizing them up and "Doc" they do look good + fine, as types.

Think this is all, seems lengthy which is as a rule considered bad taste.

We send our love to you both.

As Ever

L

P.S.
scholastic record or marks per students along with photo

TYRUS R. COBB
GLENBROOK
DOUGLAS COUNTY, NEVADA
8/30/54

Dear "Doc":-

Enclosed is letter from Mr. Candler re. James Butts your first choice.

I agree with you so heartily, all this is so worth while and so supporting to ones spirits. I have had such nice letters from several if not all that have been selected, appreciations that sound so sincere and determined as to their efforts Etc.

I am not prompting, I know you are busy and no doubt the matter is already taken care of, but I do want the pictures of those who qualified.

I wrote you about, when you needed proper funds, cash to be used as Coca cola stock is not to be sold now, I earned $500.00 the other day which goes to fund equivilent except it will go as equivilant in stock which when sold costs

no capital gains tax etc. if put
through the educational fund so
dont let me run to thin on
funds to check on.
I should I feel respond to the letters
I receive from these qualifiers, I
aim to outline a letter to each
in answer to these I have heard
from, I shall send you the copy
for your O.K. before I send etc.
Now I have heard from Aunt Nora
and that she had heard from you
I know Aunt Nora and she no
doubt had already written you
or you would not have written
her, she has been to Emory she a year or more ago
might have gotten in to you
in other words you might already
know Aunt Nora, she was there
in behalf of some student, in
need, not sure but was medicine,
Aunt Nora is quite a person a
true Cobb, (you will pardon my
briefing you) she is quite an
intellectual she can hold her
own with anyone also at any
position she might be placed in,
she has sponsored many boys and

girls, Martha Berry, Berea and
other schools of learning, she sent
me several mountain boys to
Detroit to get jobs in auto factories,
they saved all the money possible,
she fired them up for education
Etc. She has many that have gone
on to make their mark, she
has built a small so called
clinic there close to the old
Cobb home also built quite a
native stone church with organ
(pipe) Etc. she works every angle
for good of course, personally
I dont help too much, I say
I think local communities should
shoulder the cost whether if by
money or labor, also Aunt Nora
has means of her own, she
uses same some but she goes
out of her territory in her asking
Etc, if you wish to give her some
of your time ok. but do not
hesitate in not letting her absorb
your time enlist your interests
in her projects.
Aunt nora in her enthusiasm
wants to break state lines per our

set up and include the Cook home county which is in North Carolina by a very short distance, she wants to 'bend the state' line, she has written me so, as you know this should not be done, to change the set up, so you tell her, the set up and cannot be deviated from. I have had the frontal attacks for years but have "skipped the rope" many times.

She is quite a person and you may enjoy her for a while. This is all I should burden you with at present. Frances & I send our love to you both.

as Ever

2

9/4/54

Dear Doc:—

My letter of a few days ago predicated upon yours stating you would be at Lancaster for a few days then to Atlanta so this is to try and catch you in Atlanta. The inclosed is from a friend who is to my estimation a modest and unsung genius a real sincere fellow he has a son naturally this boy a genius in his mind, he could be, he also could not be, parental pride Etc. In view of past relationship I must answer Earl Bells letter and will direct him personally to you, Earl has no resources and here I say I am in no way pleading his case every person must qualify with the board of Trustees, do not judge or give his son any consideration beyond what you give others, I am only clearing myself and friendship with Earl Bell, I shall never in any way try to influence, judge the boy severely but let Earl Bell

Know I have done my part on friendship basis.

I am so pleased "Happy" has accepted, he will be a good one. Some day, let Bob Jones know about consideration of him, it will please him, also. I think it a crime the democrats used the rotten methods to one of the most perfect gentleman I have ever known, it goes to show no matter how fine, they try to crucify when one gets at the top, one is boosted up then they turn on you and try to tear you down.

Coca Cola is drifting down and for no reason, per terrific surplus also no split of stock since 1935. Bob is in a position of course to control situation of much earnings that the ordinary stock-holder has no right to participate, a selfish position as an executive, which many great businesses to day are not following, you have the situation of Montgomery Ward being challenged etc. with such a terrific surplus, sitting on selfishly refusing to let stockholders share, along with the executive boys, getting bonus of stock at preferential prices etc.

I have bought this year quite a bit of added "Coke" stock, still figuring a stock split and added stock market interest and price enhancing etc.

I have some cash that I can use to buy "Coke" as I know of only one other stock I would buy now, I then could use some of my old and cheap "Coke" stock to place for Educational Fund, the idle funds I have is too much to let be as now, some four years accumulation, I would like to buy some more "Coke" purpose as explained. The Trust Co. of Georgia really knows conditions per "Coke" for instance I dont think one would have to go high to get an inkling of conditions per "Coke" company, when we were initiating the trust fund Lawyer Smith and I think Mr. Jones of Trust dept.

and my self, I stated I did not want to have "Coke" I was putting up sold at that time as later would be better on account of possible split etc. Mr. Jones said you are right that the Trust co. was not advising anyone to sell then also Trust co. themselves was not etc. of course you knew the Trust co. is in the position to know. In my mind there is no reason in this market for Coke to sag in price except too high for buyers as they havent split there cannot be any material loss of business per the many years of operations and increases also dividends paid since 1893.

Now no one can come out cold turkey and say so & so, except R. W. W. but I thought possibly Smith or Jones of Trust dept. might give the news only by a hint, that Coke operations was normal or say well no one should sell now.

I apologize for all this and if you feel you do not want to do this, do not hesitate to decline.

I would like to buy a few hundred more shares so I can release a like amount of same stock bought cheap, to Educational Fund but I want to be sure there has been nothing drastic affecting "Coke" this year.

Also Smith or Jones or someone you might know, would give you the dope, if you told them you were "thinking" of selling some of yours.

Weather fine here, a feeling of fall in the air.

We are fine & send our love to you both.

Pardon the length of this letter.

I am, Sincerely

P.S. Hospital, Reg the Chewing profit — May – 1127⁹⁶ June – 1192¹² July 1271⁷¹

9/8/54

Dear "Doc"; -

"From one "Croney" to another high "Croney" I apoligize for flooding you with letters but this is all for good and I submit an idea to you and do not hesitate to say - no - this could be very effective if you saw fit to lend your efforts and position Etc. As I have related to you I had channelled certain fees for testimonials Etc. for quite a few years into this Educational Fund and yet I shall put plenty of my own money back of this, any fees I receive I must have come to me personally or I could not get credit for same tax wise, then I account for same and pay tax, but I use stock that cost me not too much and yes capital gains tax free Etc. Now some of these fees cause me to wonder why companys think it worth so many dollars but that is their problem, when I was fresh out of Royston just a few dollars offered, I would turn hand springs for, but now I like to shake them down for all I can especially for a good cause and also it costs me to absorb the tax Etc. these companys can charge it off.

I am enclosing a letter from one of your commercial fellow towns-man one Robert Glenn, he says he has a hell of a business, he wrote me, he called me, and I agreed to let him use the slogan "The greatest slide since Ty Cobb", no charge, now as you see he wants to dig deeper and wants my picture Etc. per Brown & Bigelow Sports Calendar and they paid me a lot of money, the contract is terminated and I can let him use this, what he wants and here I must add I have to be very careful of signed contracts and no one else is to use same for a period of time Etc. also the common use of name or testimonial Etc. by many cheapens the fee Etc. so I should benefit for all this use especially if it sends a couple of boys into higher educational schools and all so I do not think "Doc" I should

"flinch" by shaking these boys down, not that my name will help them but if they are foolish enough to pay, then I feel it Ok. its their funeral.

Now here is my plan why cant you in your position ring this fellow up, tell him you are my manager and if you tell me to do this that I will give him use of my name and picture per his letter and that Brown & Bigelow paid me several thousands of dollars, which they did, and that if he wants to use what he wants, per letter that he is doing a big business also its going into Educational Fund and we will accept $1000.00 for same, make him come out to see you and give the works to him, if this does not meet with your approval just say so and I will try him out.

I have agreed to slogan, no charge now he moves in deeper so it

should cost him.

You can impress him by saying the Life magazine stories I did, two issues, I received $25000.00 this of course went into Fund.

I think the name selected by Mrs. Eckin for the toy Greyhound perfect, he no doubt can travel fast and can line up to his name "Joy Croonay". I enclose "Happys" acceptance letter it is very good, also I return the "Joy Croonays" letter, believe me Catlett should be a real "Croonay" with all that William Fitzhugh Lee background name.

I am keeping the lable and one Luciens Beebe over in Virginia City who we missed is my meat and he could be a great "Croonay" he is a great judge of wines & food I think he would fall like a "ton of brick" though I am already in and dont have to trap him.

My idea for pictures, names & records scholasitcally of the qualifiers for Fund Etc. is to prepare a (Dossier) is this correct for a small town boy, so I can enjoy looking at it Etc.

Taylor Spink & the Mrs. may come here soon, he has evidenced the desire but Taylor has to run every detail of Sporting News and is a small spidery fellow that bellows loud, been in pain a lot with back trouble (arthritis) but what a guy and a nobleman, he would be a great "Croonay" and he is so hungry to be one. Long letters are not in good taste I apologize but I do enjoy having a seance with you via pen & paper, hope you dont mind.

Frances is in Reno lunching with some ladies we like, Dr. Strathers wife and I know she would want me to add her good wishes to "you all" I am, as Ever

Z

P.S.
This and the last letter to you — I am sure loading you up.
must tell you this — we like, have a world champion in old "Croonay chuddy, you know they do not bite they bump their adversary down and then cover them & scramble a big porcupine — I never saw so many

he man is wiser — not less than 200 — fiddles in a dog — no fooling

10/2/54

Dear "Doc":-

Enclosed will find letter
from Glenn of Atlanta, he is pledged
to $50.00 per month for three years
and he might grow, no doubt he
is small and besides he could
have had it for some time for
only $1000.00 this way we can be
assured the money he pays will
take care of possibly three but one
for each year for three years and
possibly more later as I said, I
am directing him to you now
and you can "put the works" to him
for more "if" you can, I will
ask him to call you and come to
are you so "take" care of him for
as much as you can, for we want
to school some boys as girls.
The series is a surprise to me
but Lopez, Cleveland, lost the
first game and he lost a great
advantage in a four game series,
too cautious, should have busted

68

in a run with man on third
one man down either in 6th 7th or
8th inning. Lemon held them
until 10th I believe, cautious
managing as usual in world
series, had 20 odd men on base
first two games and I think
only scored 3 runs, that
French jew Leo, has not made
a mistake or overlooked one
good move.
Hurriedly — best to "you all" from
both of us.
                as Ever
                   2

P.S. what ever you can do
shake Glenn for as much as
can and if not more o.k.
with me.
                   2
this funds are to come to me so
I can get credit income tax and
I will donate stock to fund.

ROBERT GLENN MANUFACTURING CO.

"The Greatest Slide Since Ty Cobb"

598 WELLS STREET, S.W.   •   TELEPHONE LAMAR 8284

ATLANTA, GEORGIA

September 27, 1954

Tyrus R. Cobb
Glenbrook, Douglas County
Nevada

Dear Mr. Cobb:

Thank you for your letter of the 22nd. I want you to
know that what you are doing is a great benefit to our state
and country because our young people certainly need an education to carry on our cherished traditions that are fast becoming demolished.

I am writing this letter on a letter head that I
have designed for use in our company, with our slogan "The
Greatest Slide Since Ty Cobb". That is the only wording I want
to use. In regards to the Brown & Biglow calendar, I am only
going to use about 100 of those calendars for the year 1955.
We only have about 20 customers but the Brown & Biglow representatives told me I could have 100 just as cheaply as 25, so
I took 100 for hundred dollars. It is an obsolete item with them
but they had a few left over from last year. And of course, we
can only use them for one year.

Since we are a small company and have a limited amount
of people who use our product, I should like to pay you $50.00
per month toward the great program you have created for the school
children. That will be $600.00 per year. Suppose we do this
for a three year contract and if our business grows and merits more,
then at the end of three years we will increse our offer.
If this is satisfactory to you, please send me a contract by
return mail and I will send you a check each month.

I envy you out there in that good fishing country.
When you are in Atlanta again, please come by to see us.

P.S. Get him up higher if can but close
with him an what you deem fit, show
him the boys records Etc

Yours very truly,

Robert A. Glenn

RAG/mn   Robert A. Glenn

70

7/26/56

Dear Miss McMahon;-

I want to acknowledge receipt of and thank you for your thought and kindness in sending me the material you did relative to the students who qualified and was accepted to participate in the Cobb Educational foundation for college.

You have sent me something I have for many months wanted, that is to see the pictures of the boys & girls also their records and what those in their interest for each thought of their qualifications, you have pleased me much.

You cannot imagine how much pleasure I derive from reading over these who I feel are so very close to me, also I have enjoyed showing a few of my very close friends what we are doing and the quality of these boys & girls, about all I had was some clippings and cancelled checks as evidence of my desire along these lines as above, what you have sent me brings me so very close to those that I am trying to keep and hasten to say its all very close to my heart.

Ja see the Character in the pictures also the marks as to accomplishment I feel sure we will have some real successes as men & women and that is the all thats its about. I am enjoying a great thrill and personal satisfaction.

Could I ask that you keep me up to date on the same data.

I really feel a very close & nearness to all of these boys & girls.

Thanking you, I am,

Sincerely

Ty Cobb

P.S. This naturally is a personal letter to you also has something to do in this as to your capacity as you have so much to do in selections the final screening. we like doctors much but we must have a balance many in other fields can go high in life and reflect credit toward this Foundation, even if so modest, no college or university should take the "ball" and run with it to guide to any one institution or profession. This foundation is for benefit of Georgia boys & girls who qualify as to their mark and ratings also needs and make known their desires as to institution Etc.

Think we have a fine organization board Etc. that also means you, I have an unusual regard for Dr. Caldwell with his interest and dignity.

T.R.C.

I am over stepping I know, in this. letters of inquiry after semesters of our boys & girls, if weak on some subject, a short note as to why, to the student, only to let them know we are interested & checking. Keeps them on their ~~too~~ toes and can help, not a reprimand only a prompting for those we are interested in to keep them striving, this gains success to strive.

Answer me if disposed with all confidence as being confidential, for this is all — sacred cause —

June - 10th - 57

Dear Miss McMahan:-

Yours of May, 22nd was received here upon my return from Ga, Saturday, explanation I receive my mail at Post office box Menlo Park, only a few letters slip by and is delivered to my box here at residence and evidently was here when I left for Ga. but I seldom check on this box.

This young man Selleck was over to see me yesterday, he was much pleased to read Miss Halland's letter also yours.

I appreciate your kindness in helping solve his problem, he intends to come via Georgia in Sept. also no doubt I might be in Royston at this time, I will contact you later as to arrangements you mentioned.

I have a request of you also do not let this interfere with your busy time, if possible send me a copy

---

With kindest regards to Dr. Caldwell and to you my best and with thanks for your kindness in what you have done for me.
I am,
Sincerely
Ty Cobb
T.C.

P.S.

The young man Selleck is surely intrigued with Miss Halland also her record, this boy is doing a fine work out here, holding meetings teen agers, college & outside points, he has many calls, a new Presbyterian?? church, has him employed to create interest towards members (new) for church.
T.R.C.

6/17/57

Dear Miss McMahan:-

Yours with enclosures received and want to thank you for your kindness, I enjoy these very much, sometime when can, will you send me copies of those 5 or 6 letters you let us read in the office there, one of Maddox also of Butts and one of the boy who had some offers and was delaying a year for post graduate work, was offered an instructors position to stay Etc. another I think was of a boys high honors conferred or mentioned, I like to show these to my friends as I am so proud of how everything is going with the Educational Foundation and of which you have so great a parce in.

The date July 2x th suits me, I can go to Cooperstown for July 22nd and plane down for above date, then to Royston for some house plans and back to New York for July 27.

Do not bother yourself with other data as you sent me as of July 13th unless you intend making copies for all, for I suppose we will have these copies at meeting July 24th.

---

some of the letters by or of the students along the lines of those you showed me.

Miss Slaton of Royston called on me while I was there, she is a very nice & personable girl she was selected last July, she wants to continue at Brenau I suggested she write you and give you name of her music teacher, I also met a Miss Winn she is from Vanna Ga. only about 3 miles from Royston, she is a fine type of girl, the Mayor of Royston Mr. Reeder Tucker spoke to me of her also related in same way. I believe, I suggested she write you any details relative to her work, she is an applicant I understand.

Thanking you and with kindest regards, I am,
Sincerely
Tyrus R. Cobb

TYRUS R. COBB
48 SPENCER LANE, ATHERTON
MENLO PARK, CALIFORNIA

Oct. 7, 1957.

Miss Carroll McMahon, Secy.,
Cobb Educational Fund,
244 Washington St., S. W.
Room 454,
Atlanta, (3) Georgia.

Dear Miss McMahon:

I have received report of new
students qualifying for the coming year. Your
report dated Aug. 21st, mailed Sept. 30th, is
appreciated very much.

I have just sent away part of my
belongings here by Van to Georgia so I am in the
process of moving. I have more details to contend
with which I am sending to Georgia so I can answer
when I am settled there.

I have a home rented until my real
home is completed so I shall try to have a little
time to myself in Cornelia to take care of all this.
At the present it has been a little too much for me
with all I have to do.

I am enclosing two checks, which
is a donation to the Ty Cobb Educational Fund. I do
not think that I should endorse these checks as they
will constitute a receipt from me of these funds and
will then have to be accounted for in my income tax
as checks are made out direct to Educational Fund.
some one will have to endorse these checks as the
Ty Cobb Educational Fund and not me. You or the Trust
Company of Georgia will have to endorse these checks.

We surely are thankful for this money
for a good cause. You arrange the endorsement so as to
leave me personally out of it. There should be acknowledgement made by the Educational Fund.to the real
donors , the Detroit Baseball Club, which I will furnish
you with the names at a later date which will be soon
as I am leaving here for Georgia on Wednesday or Thursday of this week.

I am enclosing letter from Detroit
and will later give you initials, etc for this formal
letter of acknowledgement of appreciation.

TYRUS R. COBB
48 SPENCER LANE, ATHERTON
MENLO PARK, CALIFORNIA

This I know is not a good letter but I am disraught with many plans here moving, etc.

With very kindest regards to Dr. Caldwell and yourself, I am

Ty Cobb

Sincerely,

ENC. 3.

My address within 4 or 5 days from date will be Cornelia, Ga.

T.R.C.

COPY

DETROIT BASEBALL COMPANY
Detroit, Michigan

John J. McHale
General Manager   September 19, 1957

Mr. Tyrus Cobb
Menlo Park, California

Dear Ty:

Enclosed please find two checks, totalling $2,647.38, representing
receipts for the Ty Cobb Night in Augusta. We are very happy to
forward these to you for your use in the Ty Cobb Foundation.

It certainly was a memorable occasion, and Messrs. Fetzer, Hansen
and the entire Detroit Baseball Company organization extend our best
wishes to you, with the hope that we will be able to see you again
soon.

                          Cordially yours,

                          John J. McHale

Checks   1 — 500.00
          1 — 2,147.38

TYRUS R. COBB
GLENBROOK, DOUGLAS COUNTY
NEVADA

5/6/58

Dear Miss McMahon:—
                Enclosed find
check please see this reaches
proper source.
I plan returning to Georgia
within 10 days and hope to contact
Dr. Caldwell and go over some
future plans relative to our
set up and get his opinion on
some matters pertaining to
future selections, and general
procedure per the Educational
Foundation.
I have searched, between here and
at Cornelia for our trust
set up drawn by Mr. Furman
Smith of Sibley, Spalding Etc.

TYRUS R. COBB
GLENBROOK, DOUGLAS COUNTY
NEVADA

offices in Trust Co. of Ga. building,
I have been unable to find same,
I am wondering if you should
know or have these papers, if
not then if Trust company,
Trust Dept. has a copy or
original, if not could you
inquire of Mr. Smith to
furnish you in your capacity
a copy, I know generally
what the set up is but want
to review same towards
making some permanent plans
as to amounts of stock or
funds to establish an amount
of income to perpetuate a
certain expenditure to accommodate
a set number of students that

TYRUS R. COBB
GLENBROOK, DOUGLAS COUNTY
NEVADA

we can afford to underwrite
in college, then I would like
to ask Dr. Caldwell to give thought
to the subject of giving preference
to male applicants over the
girl applicants, the girls are
smart and they qualify, but
they go on and a great percentage
lose their identity, marry and
lose their name, also will not
follow up in what we want
I hope Dr. Caldwell and you
will understand in my
crude way of expressing this,
I hope to explain my idea
better later, think we should
try to influence boys into
science channels and with

TYRUS R. COBB
GLENBROOK, DOUGLAS COUNTY
NEVADA

the medicine (doctors) or the
law, this to try and "take on"
boys that may go on and better
reflect credit on our Educational
Foundation, also in our
last meeting at Biltmore I
sensed that better judgments
thought we should select
students only from an
accredited School.
There are these matters I would
like to discuss with Dr.
Caldwell.
Please overlook such a lengthy
letter.
I am,
                    Sincerely
                    Ty Cobb

C. N. Weatherly Company

INCORPORATED
"COMPLETE HOME FURNISHERS"
FURNITURE · ELECTRICAL APPLIANCES · JEWELRY
ROYSTON, GEORGIA

Saturday

Dear Miss McMahon:-

Enclosed are some of the
letters I have received, not all as I have quite
a lot of mail which has accumulated and
some havent opened, I am handicapped as
to answering as I am in a "rat race" trying
to accomadate many requests.

After I was in Atlanta when I was last
there and came to your office, I realized
I was to come on Friday not Thursday, I do
hope I did not compromise Dr. Caldwells plans
by this mistake of mine, I had to attend an
American Legion meeting Thursday night and
had previously planned to stay the night and
come to see you & Dr. Caldwell next day but
some people here who offered to drive me to
Atlanta had to come back Thursday night so

C. N. WEATHERLY
PRESIDENT

W. B. WELLBORN
MANAGER

STORES AT:

ROYSTON, GA.

HARTWELL, GA.

C. N. Weatherly Company

INCORPORATED
"COMPLETE HOME FURNISHERS"
FURNITURE · ELECTRICAL APPLIANCES · JEWELRY
ROYSTON, GEORGIA

that explains the mistake mistake I made.
The Life magazine man there in Atlanta who
wanted the story with details of the set up
of Educational Fund which would correct
the garbled story by Herald - Telegram paper
N.Y. And that has caused a confusion
also the result has been, all these letters I
enclose to come to me, so if you can reach
this Life magazine reporter at Jackson - 2-9233
have him come over and you give him all
details of our set up, then possibly these people
would write direct to your office.
Am sorry to load all this upon you but I
want to be relieved of having to reply to
them.

Sincerely
L. Cobb

I am,

P.S. am leaving for California Tuesday or Wednesday - be there for several weeks - Menlo Park, Calif.

Cornelia   **TYRUS R. COBB**   7/28/58
ROYSTON, GEORGIA

Dear Miss McMahon:-
       I plan on being
at meeting July 31ˢᵗ at the
set time.
    Hope will have copy of our
Trust set up, I received one
but per flood of mail and
a short time effort to find
it havent located but expect
to make a very thorough search
hope am successful.
    I simply have no filing facilities
nor any one to file, so bear
with me in my travail.
I am.
         Sincerely
         Ty Cobb

WESTERN UNION
TELEGRAM

W. P. MARSHALL, PRESIDENT

1201

The filing time shown in the date line on domestic telegrams is STANDARD TIME at point of origin. Time of receipt is STANDARD TIME at point of destination

AB607 OB247

O CYA058 NL PD=CACARSON CITY NEV 29=   1958 AUG 29 PM 8 49

MISS CARROLL MCMAHON=

    244 WASHINGTON ST SOUTHWEST RM 454 ATLANTA GA=

=MY SELECTION NUMBERS ONE TWO THREE FOUR NINE TEN TWELVE
FOURTEEN FIFTEEN SIXTEEN AND SEVENTEEN. LIST FOR
SELECTION FOLLOWS AIR MAIL=

    =T R COBB==.

THE COMPANY WILL APPRECIATE SUGGESTIONS FROM ITS PATRONS CONCERNING ITS SERVICE

TYRUS R. COBB
GLENBROOK, DOUGLAS COUNTY
NEVADA

8/28/58

Dear Miss McMahan:

am very sorry about
this being late, hope arrives in
time.

Think we should give boys preference
also lean towards science.

Have done this very crudely, I have
not been well, had a very
trying trip out by auto, long
distance also very hot.

My address will be Menlo Park,
Calif. as I am to be there for a
few days. then back here to rest
up. but Menlo Park will be
forwarded if should not be there.

Kindest regards to Dr. Caldwell
and yourself, I am,

Sincerely
Ty Cobb

TYRUS R. COBB
GLENBROOK, DOUGLAS COUNTY
NEVADA

10/10/58

Dear Miss McMahan:-

First is enclosed a
check for Trust Co. to be credited
to Educational Fund.
First I am feeling so much
better tension wise and as to
general health, I am launched on
a fine system of conditioning.
doctors, bath + massage also road
work which am much pleased
per results, I am on Lake Tahoe
with plenty of room away from
cities Etc. Briefly my case is a
very (or was) highly developed one
of Tension.

One question please advise me
of the new students accepted how
many was on my selected list.
I tried to convey that the girl from
Emmanuel School or college, near
Royston Ga, my home, this is an
Holiness School or college, she might
deserve her High marks also she
might not in comparison to other
more higher rated o institutions,
So because one is from Royston

Georgia area, my home, they should
not be shown any preference, I
say all this to you to be conveyed
to Dr. Caldwell.
I tried to express myself as being
in full accord with what I think
is of Dr. Caldwell's mind also yours
per selection from accredited
institutions, there are so many
fine deserving students whose
marks were gained in a higher
and more difficult institution,
(ink refill wrong color) and some
are shut out in our selection
in favor of less deserving, I hope
am wrong and if so I am sorry, but
I feel the girl from Emanuel,
Royston, Ga. should have no special
message commending her on her
high marks. etc.
The question of finances were mentioned
I stated that was my obligation and
would surely be taken care of, it was,
and for Dr. Caldwell and your
information only, in this year and
before 1959, the Educational Foundation
with the Trust co. of Georgia, will
have a very appreciable amount of
money or stocks at their disposal

for future use, I do not think my
position as donor and my plans
of procedure per my desire and wish
be questioned, this happens to be
my obligation and I do have a
deep feeling relative to any obligation
or desires that I initiate, I do
get a deep sense of happiness in
what I am doing, I do hope we
can all carry on for what I think
is a fine thing, and am being
bold enough to say, if we have the
fine cooperation we have had in
the past, we will surely score
highly in our endeavors. I am
very deeply appreciative of so much
fine unselfishness of those who
are connected with this project.
I feel highly honored your request
in behalf of the Barnes boys, I hope
am fulfilling your desires in the
way they want it, so I enclose two
cards.
I know Dr. Caldwell is burdened
for his duties and I ask that you submit
anything in my letters to him that
I write of, I will not express in this what
I think of him.   Sincerely
I am, — No stenographer terrible letter. Ty Cobb

TYRUS R. COBB
48 SPENCER LANE, ATHERTON
MENLO PARK, CALIFORNIA

529

5/24/59

Dear Miss McMahan!—
            Enclosed find check
for Educational Foundation, first
time in my life a recompense
for a number of balls to be
autographed & returned, a promotion
project in entertaining, this
company's field organization.
Please write Mr. Taylor and
acknowledge, address & co., enclosed.
Dr. Kennedy, will write you about
arrangement of date in Atlanta
for Educational Fund meeting
his aim is to attend, he also
must attend Regents of University
of Michigan, meeting, date not
officially decided, he thinks July
24th will advise later, I must be
in Cooperstown, N.Y. annual
celebration of Baseball's Hall of Fame,
19th — 20 & 21st of July, also these
dates were accepted in April, I
have invited Dr. Kennedy and he can
make Cooperstown and return to
Detroit for Regents meeting, if consistent
with Dr. Caldwell to have our

meeting in Atlanta say July
16th or 17th, this of course is tentative
until we know date of Dr. Kennedys
regents meeting.
Regards to Dr. Caldwell, I am
                    Sincerely
                    Ty Cobb

May 26, 1959

Miss Carroll McMahon
Cobb Educational Foundation
20 Ivy St. S. E.
Atlanta 3, Georgia

Dear Miss McMahon:

You will recall that on May 11th I wrote you a
note stating that following the Regents Meeting last
week I would give you a definite date which would be
most convenient for me to attend the Cobb Foundation
Meeting in July. Mr. Cobb has said that he would like
me to join him on a trip to Cooperstown on July 22 and
23rd. There has been no final decision by the Regents
regarding a July Meeting in Ann Arbor, so I have decided to set aside the week of July 20th to 25th and
will be glad to meet with all of you in Atlanta on the
20th, 21st, 24th or 25th. If you will let me know
what date fits in with your schedule, I will be governed according.

With every good wish,

Sincerely yours,

Chas. S. Kennedy.

Charles S. Kennedy, M.D.

CSK/mo

9/28/59

Dear Miss McMahon:-

Enclosed find check for Educational Foundation.

Was pleased to see Dr. Caldwell looking so well after surgery Etc.

Am getting rested up after trip, in this nice cool weather.

I am,

Sincerely

T. R. Cobb

P.S. If we have some students studying for the ministry please give me names and records Etc. have a small donation for too,

T.R.C.

10/12/59

Dear Miss McMahon;—

As you see I am returning the transcripts for your files, No doubt you wondered my request and I must, I feel explain and you can tell Dr. Caldwell but no one else as I do not seek credit.

This is an unusual and rather a sacred revealing, I happen to be rather serious along certain lines, also its the way to happiness or peace of mind in our declining years.

I cashed a $200.00 check for a person, the check was misplaced or lost in my possession, I wrote and asked only for a duplicate, this person had evidenced or claimed a religious or Christian ~~attitude~~ attitude, upon my request for a duplicate check, I was much surprised to be told, well its your hard luck & your loss, the only thing I could say was well if that is your attitude and you claim

TYRUS R. COBB
48 SPENCER LANE, ATHERTON
MENLO PARK, CALIFORNIA

a Christian spirit, if you have a conscience, you will be burdened a long time, after that I prayed quite a bit, but this was a selfish prayer, I asked God that this person would have revealed to them the wrong of it and also promised if I received this small amount due me, that I would use it in some way for Gods work, & to keep me in a few days I am called on phone, and they were sending me another check, I received it and cashed it, so these two boys in Devinity schools are receiving now in the mail, one hundred dollars each, extra to what we are giving them. So think this over, I am allowed a real happiness in this act, I think this way is so very right. My regards to Dr. Caldwell. I am,

Sincerely
Ty Cobb

Trust co., has a very sizeable amount as surplus, now.

TYRUS R. COBB
ROYSTON, GEORGIA 12/5/59

Dear Miss McMahon:—
                    Another check
for Educational Foundation,
I will or should be in Atl'outa
before you receive this, I shall
call Dr. Caldwell when I get
settled there for a few days.
Leaving here tonight shortly
after midnight.
I am,
                    Sincerely
                    Ty Cobb

90

Cobb Memorial Hospital

Royston, Georgia

MRS. CARL REEVES, R. N.
Superintendent

1/17/60

Dear Miss McMahon:-

Enclosed find check for our Educational Foundation also wish you to make formal acknowledgement to Mr. Kase, on his position also wish you to know this was not an exaction on my part but a proposal or free will offer from Mr. Kase, in behalf of B'nai B'rith organization for "my appearance to be honored".

Might see Dr. Caldwell & yourself some day of the coming week,

I am,

Sincerely

Ty Cobb

P.S. I have a real prospect for next year a young man who qualifies, been 3 years Inland, had to stop to earn by teaching school in Cornelia Ga, to finish Etc. I like the idea of knowing

the progress per semester as you recently
sent to me,

Am not a patient here, rest and proper
schedule carrying out process, close to
Emory doctors also N.Y. where I have
to go Jan 28th + 31st then back to Emory
for final decisions etc,

T.R.C.

TYRUS R. COBB
48 SPENCER LANE, ATHERTON
MENLO PARK, CALIFORNIA

3/2/60

Dear Miss McMahon:-

Here is a small check, you might acknowledge this with expression of appreciation, this is a Jewish club, just address this way, B'nai Brith, Boston Sports Lodge, Boston Mass. they can use as evidence in charge off Etc.

I am feeling fairly well, sorry I missed seeing you, I appreciate very much your thought in calling, Kindest to Dr. Caldwell, Iam,

Sincerely
Ty Cobb

P.S.

Miss Templeton called to see me she is a student at Emory, a very impressive fine little girl, I would say we are complimented to have her.   T.R.C.

Jimmy Butts called on me several times, he is very popular and scoring very well.—   T.R.C.

TYRUS R. COBB
48 SPENCER LANE, ATHERTON
MENLO PARK, CALIFORNIA

5/26/60

Dear Miss McMahon:-

Just an answer to yours of May 16th. Think at least applicants could do would be the photo in future and those who havent gone to the little trouble in securing & submitting with application and those who havent, that this is a must and would like you to stress this in future, no photo, no consideration, Miss McMahon we are entitled to see and size up applicants, for instance strength and good quality's reflected in ones face goes far, thats Why big corporations have personel dept. and trained ones at that, to see the person to note habits of use of hands, their strong face, also when they approach personel man or woman, they are being sized up how they are dressed how they walk even, their attention and acts (unconscious) is being measured, and when they

walk away after interview is being
observed, until then only, possibly
a push of a button might indicate
a decision, we must have
photographs, proper size etc. acts
during interview under these conditions
big corporations, their trained personel
man or woman oft swings the
scales and most important a photo
is very much in the picture,
lets stress this and bring all
brochures up to date, insist.
I was complimented and honored to
have a very fine girl, my guess, come
and call on me in Emory hospital,
my room, she was a coed there, I
had never seen her, she lives at
Blythe, Ga. close to augusta where
I lived, we had chosen her she
was one of ours, there she presented
herself and to my judgement
about the finest little gal I have
seen, she seems to really have all
it takes, a perfect little person as
a female, wide eyes a fine little
lady, serious, wish she was my

daughter, though mine are really tops, both now married, this girl is Miss Templeton I think is her name. we want all of them to submit pictures, I personally know of few as to what they show in their face. it would help a lot for all to submit pictures in our decision to accept them, further if we have the number thats graduating, we will have to choose quite a few, if the crops should not be so good, we are not wedded to any number to accept, but I am sort of fixing 36 in number of boys & girls that I can continue to help, also have things worked out. Mr. Parks, I want you to feel that I now know close to amount of money or securities to Trust say that properly handled will endow this Educational Foundation to carry on in perpetuity, this is to be done within this year. I am going to build a 5 room house in Cornelia Ga. this

year, not a large house I had plans & specifications for as of last year, on property I have there for this reason but changed my mind on the largeness of house for servants I found there an impossible matter, hence my change of mind, this smaller house is to be erected this year, I am donating my house here above address to Educational Foundation and sold all proceeds to Educational foundation, to eliminate a considerable capital gains tax, this amount to be a part of my funds to endow Etc. I ask you to submit this letter, my plans to Dr. Caldwell, he is busy, I know and this long hand writing is a task so I feel this a better, most of this letter to you is for him to know about, much labor by me to save.

Now your letter per being finished with applicants and a meeting any time after middle of June, I have work laid out out here in June that I cannot be there until well into July. then I can came as I intend going to Cooperstown N.Y.

again, this will be late in July, so I can come there from my duties out here, then come there attend our meeting. then Royston Hospital Trustee meeting, then to Cooperstown, further am now planning to attend Olympics in Rome. about aug 15th to Sept 15th back in this country for baseball finishes per pennant and then World Series in Oct. then after that I have free time Etc. I am not well also not really sick, though much in travail, after my operation there in Emory, I was placed on a line of medication would to term it a cleansing and trying to eliminate the causes of my operation which relieved me much, these medicines is what causes me now a much underpar feelings, I am "wailing" about, so not too serious. so not to serious my age of 73 am or have not in all my life been used to the underpar feelings. I hope I am making all this understandable,

I shall indicate, later, when I can be there to participate in our meeting, as before stated in July.

Our Jimmy Butts a wonderful boy, graduates in June, he has so informed me by invitation I would surely like to be there but impossible, this boy being in Emory came to see me in sick room in hospital many times, he my guess will go high in his life to live. if you havent seen in person Miss Templeton, the co ed at Emory, and you havent too much to do in your duties, could call her and ask she come to see you & Dr. Caldwell. am sure you would enjoy an interview and of course, anything you wish to say or advise, might be quite an inspiration for this girl, for she is from the "sticks" and might reverence this personal talk, per her future and aims.

Our star as of now Jerry Sutton at Johns Hopkins is some young and is bound to go high, a very recent letter to me, seems to indicate this young man, after last summer at Los Alamos, research, has now made up 2 years of work at Johns Hopkins, no less, and they are now there offering him a profership when he graduates, these matters thrill me, Miss McMahon and Dr. Caldwell. I hope we can take care of him even more substantially in our next meeting. Long letters are not in proper form, I am sorry for the implication, but even so I enjoy the labor of writing all this, yes we have others but cannot cope with all of each of our boys & girls.

I am, with best wishes for you & Dr. Caldwell, I am,

Sincerely
T. Cobb

P.S. The boy at Tulane for his last year, is another to watch, can't remember his name.

up to date, think if you can, to carry Ellis + Rankin, as deceased etc.

These who have disqualified + put on waiver + the other men, such being all this

My address very soon now, Glenbrook, Nevada, for weeks. P.C. but some new stationary, leaving, of Chandler and off

(over)

97

I have after finishing this jumbled letter, that you have thought of and have the proper change of stationery heading. Thanks
T.R.C.

6/14/60

Dear Miss McMahan;—

previous letter you stated you Think am right that in could hold meeting or set same, early, possibly in June, recent developments, it would suit me perfectly if it could be arranged to meet in Atlanta, Cobb Educational foundation to select qualifiers for next year, I can leave here anytime now for this meeting, in fact it will help me much, my plans, so you & Dr. Caldwell set any date say June 20th or up to June 25th or if inconvenient July 1st or 2nd. and please advise me quick, Menlo Park, Calif, and mark hold, I have two

99

TYRUS R. COBB
GLENBROOK, DOUGLAS COUNTY
NEVADA

meeting, both a must, Royston
Cobb memorial Hospital and
Educational Foundation, Atlanta, Ga.
am trying to work in to attend
Baseballs Hall of Fame meeting
Cooperstown, N.Y. Its June
27th to clean up my plans to
follow in the east.

Do let me know your decision
per date Educational Foundation
meeting — quick.

I am,

Sincerely
Ty Cobb

air mail

ZEPHYR COVE
1960
JUN 15
5 PM
NEV.

Miss Carolyn McMahon,
244 Washington, S. W.
Room 454, Atlanta, (3)
Ga.

TYRUS R. COBB
GLENBROOK, DOUGLAS COUNTY
NEVADA

Nov - 5 - 60

Dear Miss McMahon;—
Just a few lines to keep
in contact Etc.
First subject, while in Emory Hospital
a very fine person as one of our students
came up to see me Miss Templeton
from Blythe, Ca. impressed me very much
a very fine young lady, made me wish
much that I had a son that could have
interested her.
Miss Theresa Gailey was accepted there
at Emory, I thought it would be fine if
these two girls could know each other, also
as Templeton was more advanced than my
cousin Miss Gailey, her father and I was
down to Emory and tried to locate Miss
Templeton and have them meet as if
friendship had matured. Miss Templeton
could assist my cousin over and rough
spots etc. we could not locate Templeton
they knew her, seemed she was assigned to
some Hall Etc. I wrote her to Blythe, Ca.
her home and asked letter be forwarded
a considerable time passed, I finally
received a wedding announcement,
address I believe Nashville Tenn.
I thought I would bring this to your
attention, I in no way think or believe
Miss Templeton has not reported this to
you, so she could be eliminated from
our sponsorship, please advise me of this.

I am not real happy from a physical
standpoint even if I did take off from
hospital out here for Olympic games
my back pains are still much in
evidence, my only surcease is Codeine.
Etc. My hospital visit was for mechanical
treatments, a series which am told will
have to keep up at intervals Etc. hence
the liberty of trip to Rome Etc.
I am busy here on Lake Tahoe where
it is quiet, am working with
collaborator on my book, am sure
happy I did not "drag" Dr. Caldwell
into this, time, and mass of work,
research Etc. rehashing, polishing
up, meetings with publishers, would
have been too much, I am now sorry
I went into it, also have learned there
is not too much to gain authoring
books for publishers, please tell
Dr. this, would write him but he
I feel is too busy coping with my
letters Etc.
We have had two snows, not of any
real depth, they clear away quickly and
then this glorious Lake Tahoe and also
pleasant weather, but the real thing is
coming, any time, unpredictable. I

am holding myself ready to leave by
auto Etc. for Georgia, I have some plans
there that I must meet & carry out I
expect to be there until I go to Phoenix
Ariz. for that fine & mild climate.
My address for enough time for you
to answer this will be Glenbrook,
Nevada, Douglas Co.,—
Kindest regards to Dr. + your self,
Jam,
Sincerely,
Ty Cobb

P.S. I hear from some who seem
appreciate also of progress, but not
too many. Fine reports from
Sutton (Jerry) Johns Hopkins from
men of that institution and
surely not solicited.
To follow proper TRC
course and for creation of a real
cause, swish, if we have any, that slow
up and rest too much on their oars and
hold our keep cheaply, that they be warned
also if fail to heed and marks sag at end
of school year — let's drop them. TRC.

P.S. My stay in
Ga. will be to carry
out the endowment
of Cobb Educational
Foundation.

T.R.C.

TYRUS R. COBB
~~GLENBROOK - DOUGLAS COUNTY~~
~~NEVADA~~
2/25/61

Cornelia. Ga.

Dear Miss M'Mahan:-

Your letter recieved relative to Jack Colwell and I certainly concur with your idea of dropping him, he sounds like a first class "leaner", the first paragraph his letter our reinstatement lines doesnt ring so good. No need to give Colwell my address, if write him say that I 'divest myself of all correspondence I can. I do not like to interfere in any way any dicisions or actions of the Foundation. I am very well doing so

TYRUS R. COBB
GLENBROOK, DOUGLAS COUNTY
NEVADA

well as should expect, will
say I am not exactly enjoying
your Ga. weather.

I am leaving around Mch.
1st for Phoenix Ariz. for a
month or more, My address
there will be Safari Hotel.
then after say April 8th I
will be at Menlo Park, Calif.
then back here after 2 or 3
weeks.

With kindest regards, I am,

4/20/61

Dear Miss McMahon;–

The enclosed is self explanatory, dont think she will have to be accorded any special consideration, but to be sure I would like her receive same, if her marks Etc. merit it.

Am out here attending some matters and expect to return to Ga. (Cornelia) for quite a stay. Cornelia

This Loudermilk boy, is another one I wish to be accepted if his marks warrant, need not investigate family financial position, I now them well, fine mother and father, lots of adversity.

Kindest to Dr. Caldwell, I am,

Sincerely
Ty Cobb

P.S.

Please notify Dr. Kennedy and of course the other members of board, to attend this coming meeting a must, I have some director Medallions to present

T.R.C.

merely state it is my particular desire all Directors be there this particular time

CHAPTER FOUR

The Scholarship Board

The persons to whom such scholarships shall be furnished shall be selected by a Scholarship Board consisting originally of Dr. Daniel C. Elkin, Dr. Harmon Caldwell, Dr. Fred W. Rankin, and Mrs. Tyrus R. Cobb.

– ITEM II of the official Charter for the Ty Cobb Educational Fund, dated December 30, 1953.

Records don't show exactly how Ty Cobb perceived the idea of starting an educational fund for Georgia residents. But, documents are available that indicate his deep desire to provide college assistance to bright and deserving students.

"It is my hope that this fund will constitute a permanent fund and that eventually the income only will be used for scholarships," Cobb said in the official charter of the Foundation. "However, I realize that during the first few years until the income is sufficient to provide one or more scholarships, it will be necessary for the Scholarship Board to use principal for the purpose of providing scholarships, and for this reason, the Scholarship Board is not restricted to use the income only for that purpose."

Making sure that all the bases were covered, Cobb also set forth: "In all matters a decision of a majority of said Board shall control, and the Trustee (Trust Company of Georgia, which was designated to manage the fund)

shall be authorized to act on any paper signed by a majority of the Board as constituting the act of the Board."

And he also knew that the membership of the Board would change through the years. "Should a vacancy occur in said Board through death, resignation, or failure to act, then the remaining members or member of said Board shall designate a successor or successors who shall have all the rights, powers and duties of the original members of said Board. Should said remaining members or member for any reason fail to appoint successors, so that there are no qualified members of said Board, then the Judge of the Superior Court of Franklin County, Georgia, on the application of the Trustee (Trust Company of Georgia) or any person therein interested, shall appoint such successors." *(Taken from the official Charter of the Ty Cobb Educational Fund.)*

It's obvious that Cobb wanted responsible people to manage his new scholarship fund, but it isn't all that obvious how he selected the very first Board.

How he came to know Daniel C. Elkin, M.D., who was professor of surgery at Emory University Hospital in 1953, isn't quite clear. Perhaps Dr. Elkin had been Cobb's doctor, or a family member's surgeon. It is, however, very clear that Cobb made a great selection in his choice of Dr. Elkin to head up the first Scholarship Board of the Ty Cobb Educational Fund, later to be known as the Ty Cobb Educational Foundation.

Dr. Elkin was a big name in the Atlanta medical community. He had assumed the chairmanship of the department of surgery at Emory University in 1930, and due to a substantial endowment to establish a chair of surgery, was named the first Joseph Brown Whitehead Professor of Surgery in 1939.

Through his innovative contributions to the developing fields of vascular and trauma surgery, Dr. Elkin solidified the department's position of surgical practice and research, and also improved the surgical curriculum at Emory.

Emory publications report that during the decade following World War II, the department of surgery had emerged from largely a volunteer-based faculty to one composed of academic members. During the war, Dr. Elkin served as commanding general of Ashford General Hospital in West Virginia, the largest of four army hospitals designated as vascular centers. After the war, he returned to Emory and was instrumental in changing the teaching facilities from Grady Hospital to the Emory campus. After years of negotiations, The Emory Clinic was opened in January 1953, apparently about the same time that

Dr. Elkin's letter-writing days were set to begin with Ty Cobb.

Another original selection to the Board was Dr. Harmon W. Caldwell, chancellor of the University System of Georgia who would later become chairman of the board when Dr. Elkin passed away in 1958. The reason for choosing Dr. Caldwell isn't clear from the Foundation records, but he may have been Dr. Elkin's selection because of his educational background. However, Cobb also knew him.

Mrs. Gwendolyn Caldwell, who married Harmon Caldwell in December 1944, remembers a late-night phone call her husband received about a year following their marriage. Then the president of the University of Georgia in Athens, Dr. Caldwell answered the phone about 2:00 A.M. "I heard him say 'no' two or three times before finally saying 'no Ty, I can't do that'," she recalled.

It seems that Ty Cobb was trying to persuade the UGA President to purchase some Coca-Cola stock to make some money for the University. "He told Harmon that Coca-Cola was going to jump way up and that he would loan him the money to purchase the stock," Mrs. Caldwell remembered. "He (Cobb) said that if it made

Cobb, Joe Jackson, and Sam Crawford before a game in Cleveland, 1912.

money he (Dr. Caldwell) could pay him back, but that if it didn't pay off, it would be his (Cobb's) loss," she said.

So, as early as 1945, Dr. Caldwell knew Ty Cobb well enough to talk with him over the phone in the middle of the night. Cobb apparently was calling from his California home, and was paying little attention to the time difference.

Still, Mrs. Caldwell didn't know exactly how her husband and Cobb originally met. "I guess it was through baseball," she said.

Mrs. Caldwell remembers Ty Cobb as a "very kind man" who "always invited me to attend the Foundation's luncheons and annual meetings." Most meetings, she said, were held at the Capital City Club in downtown Atlanta.

"One reason I liked Ty Cobb so much," she said, "was because he always acted like a gentleman." She said that the Trustees made recommendations for scholarship recipients, but Ty "made up his own mind...he had to go over everything himself before decisions were made."

A graduate of Harvard Law School, Dr. Caldwell was appointed an assistant professor of law at Emory University in 1924 and may have known Dr. Elkin at that time. He joined the faculty at the University of Georgia as a professor of law in 1929, became dean of the Law School in 1933, and two years later Dr. Caldwell was named president of the University, a position he held through 1948.

In 1949, Dr. Caldwell became the third UGA president to be named chancellor of the University System of Georgia. He presided over a decade of slow but steady growth in the 1950s, an era marked by an increase in building projects and faculty salaries.

As in the case of Dr. Elkin, it is also perfectly clear that the naming of Dr. Caldwell was an important selection for the up-and-coming scholarship foundation.

A third member of the original board was to be a lawyer from Royston with the last name of Johnson. In a seven-page handwritten letter to Dr. Elkin from his home in Menlo Park, California, addressed "Dear Doc" and dated November 13, 1953, Cobb rambled about naming Johnson to the board, "more of a friendly gesture honor to him, etc."

However, Cobb became aggravated with Johnson and took his name off the list. *(See story on page 12 in Chapter 2 - Getting Started - and full letter on pages 20-23.)*

So, as it turned out, the third member of the original scholarship Board turned out to be Dr. Fred Rankin of Lexington, Kentucky, who had served as president of the American College of Surgeons and as president of the American Medical Association. It isn't clear through retained documents exactly how Dr. Rankin became a member, but one would guess that he was a friend of Dr. Elkin, who also had a home and later moved to Lancaster, Kentucky, a small town located a few miles south of Lexington. Perhaps Dr. Rankin also had served as Cobb's doctor somewhere along the way.

The fourth and final member of the original Board was Mrs. Tyrus R. Cobb – Frances Fairburn Cobb – the second wife of the baseball great. When Frances Cobb turned the key at the formal opening of the Cobb Memorial Hospital in Royston in January 1950, the attractive 40-year-old brunette had been married to Cobb only four months. Then 62, Cobb's new wife was the daughter of John Fairburn, a Buffalo, New York, physician whom Cobb had known for some years.

So now, the stage was set for the late November 1953 announcement of the Foundation.

Membership of the Board changed quickly the next year. It is not completely clear whether Dr. Fred Rankin, who, as previously mentioned, lived in Kentucky, attended the announcement of the new Cobb Foundation in Atlanta. A letter from Dr. Elkin to Dr. Rankin, dated December 3, 1953, in fact, indicated that Dr. Rankin did not attend. It said: "Everything went off well here, and Ty is getting his foundation started. I will keep in touch with you about its progress."

The Board announced its first scholarship recipients in a press release dated August 16, 1954. *(See pages 34-35 in Chapter 3 - The Fund.)* The last statement in the release read: "Announcement of the scholarship winners is made by Dr. Daniel C. Elkin, Chairman of the Board of Trustees; Mrs. Tyrus R. Cobb and Dr. Harmon Caldwell, Trustees."

Thus, although there is no documentation of when Dr. Rankin apparently had passed away prior to the first meeting of the board. In a letter from Dr. Elkin to the Hon. Albert B. Chandler of Versailles, Kentucky, dated two days prior to the press release (August 14, 1954), he said: "I am sorry, my dear Governor, that I had to see you under such trying circumstances on the last occasion of our meeting. I know how dear Fred was to you."

Dr. Elkin was providing information to Governor Chandler about the Foundation, in hopes that Chandler would join the Board of Trustees: "The terms of Mr. Cobb's foundation also provide that the trustees shall be self-perpetuating. In case of the death or resignation of any trustee, the other trustees will select a successor. After a conference with Mrs. Cobb and Dr. Caldwell, we have decided to ask you to serve as successor to Dr. Rankin."

Completing his pitch, Dr. Elkin wrote: "We feel that you would be an excellent choice for several reasons. We know of your long and intimate friendship with Dr. Rankin and of your friendship and admiration for Mr. Cobb who has done this fine thing for education. Moreover, we are cognizant of your own particular interest in education."

Then, in a copy of a press release dated on September 8, 1954, it was official: "The Honorable Albert B. (Happy) Chandler of Versailles, Kentucky, has been elected Trustee of the Cobb Educational Foundation, succeeding Dr. Fred W. Rankin of Lexington, Kentucky."

Happy Chandler was a big name, not only in Kentucky but throughout the baseball world. He had served as governor of the Bluegrass State (1935-39), senator of Kentucky (1939-45) and commissioner of baseball (1944-51). He would be elected governor again in 1955, holding the office through 1959.

"I feel greatly honored by the suggestion that I become a trustee of the foundation set up by my friend, Ty Cobb," Chandler wrote in an August 23, 1954, letter to Dr. Elkin. "You also honor me by letting me serve in place of our dear departed mutual friend, Dr. Fred Rankin. I will try to be as helpful as he would have been because I know of his great interest in this project."

The Kentuckian added: "I, too, am sorry, my dear friend, that we met under such trying circumstances recently. I know how much Fred meant to you and of course my family and I are almost completely lost in bewilderment because of his death."

Governor Chandler was a major addition to the board in many ways. In an August 26, 1954, letter from Dr. Caldwell to Miss Alice Merchant, secretary to Dr. Elkin and the first secretary of the Ty Cobb Educational Foundation, Dr. Caldwell related: "I am delighted to

know that Mr. Chandler has consented to serve as a Trustee of the Cobb Educational Foundation. I believe that he can be of material assistance to us. Furthermore, this will give me the opportunity to renew an association that was begun when Mr. Chandler and I were freshmen together at the Harvard Law School."

Ty Cobb himself also was involved in the selection of Chandler to the Board, although apparently not as an active member of the process...it was hard to tell by the letters. In an August 21, 1954, letter to Dr. Elkin – "Dear Doc" – from his home in Douglas County, Nevada, Cobb wrote: "I like your idea of 'Hap.' I like him. Should there be any unforeseen or reason he could not accept, and really 'Doc' I had not thought of any other course since you were here...should Happy have some reason, and I am sure he won't, then let's think of 'Bob' Jones and Senator George who I know very well."

Cobb rambled on during the six-page handwritten letter, and never returned to the topic of Happy Chandler, Bob Jones or Senator George. (*See letter on pages 57-59 of Chapter 3 - The Fund.*)

However, in another letter to "Doc" dated September 4, 1954, Cobb returned to the subject of Chandler and Jones. "I am pleased Happy has accepted, he will be a good one. Someday let Bob Jones know about consideration of him, it will please him." Later in the letter he moved into a long story about "Coke" stock and mentioned Mr. Jones of the trust department of Trust Company of Georgia. (*See letter on pages 64-65 of Chapter 3 - The Fund.*)

It is not clear if "Bob Jones" was the same person as the great golfer from Georgia whose life (1902-1971) and career were almost parallel with those of Cobb (Cobb retired from baseball in 1928 and Jones retired from competitive golf in 1930). It is a fact, however, that Cobb and Bobby Jones played a lot of golf together. One book reported that Jones, who was the number-one amateur golfer of his time, gave lessons to Cobb. There is a photo on record, as well as a photo of Cobb, Jones, sports writer Grantland Rice, and another (unknown) amateur golfer following the 1928 U.S. Amateur Golf Tournament.

The "Senator George" mentioned undoubtedly was Sen. Walter F. George (1879-1957) who served alongside Sen. Richard B. Russell, Jr. for a number of years as U.S. senators from Georgia. No mention is made if the two were actually recruited as Board members of the

Foundation, but neither ever served.

The foursome of Dr. Elkin, Mrs. Cobb, Dr. Caldwell, and Mr. Chandler met on the Emory University campus on July 21, 1955, and selected the second set of scholarship recipients – four renewals and seven new students.

Later that year, another change took place on the Board.

"I herewith resign as Trustee of the Cobb Educational Fund effective this date, December 7, 1955," Frances F. Cobb wrote to Dr. Elkin from her Reno, Nevada, home. It isn't mentioned in the communications, but Frances Cobb, who married Cobb on September 24, 1949, had filed for divorce in September 1955, a request that would be granted in May 1956.

In a letter dated a week later from Dr. Elkin to Dr. Caldwell, the chairman noted the resignation of Frances Cobb and asked: "What is your personal opinion about appointing Earl Mann to the vacancy. I think Ty would approve of this action. In fact, I am sure he would approve of any action we take."

There is no documentation in the files about what happened next, but Earl Mann was never named to the Board. Instead, a baseball great by the name of Earle Combs from Richmond, Kentucky, was named to replace Mrs. Cobb.

Combs, a Yankee for 12 years, never played with Cobb in the major leagues, but did go against him while playing as a star with the New York Yankees. Also a centerfielder, Combs had led off the famous "Murderer's Row" batting order for the Yankee teams of the 1920s and early 1930s, batting in front of Babe Ruth and Lou Gehrig. Cobb would have been very pleased with baseball's veterans committee when "The Kentucky Colonel" was selected to the Hall of Fame in 1970, nine years after Cobb's death.

Ty Cobb himself, along with Dr. Charles S.

Cobb at opening day of the 1925 World Series.

Kennedy of Detroit, also joined the Board that year. Dr. Kennedy was a member of the Board of Regents of the University of Michigan, and, although not documented, probably became friends with the Georgian when Cobb played for the Detroit Tigers.

The "new" six-member Board, including Dr. Elkin (who by this time was listed as Professor Emeritus), Dr. Caldwell, Mr. Chandler, Mr. Combs, Dr. Kennedy, and Ty Cobb, met in Atlanta on June 30, 1956, to award the third "class" of scholarships.

At some point during the ensuing months, Dr. Elkin apparently moved to Kentucky, but retained his position as Chairman of the Board. A letter is on file from Dr. Caldwell to Dr. Elkin, dated March 21, 1956, to Elkin Place, Lancaster, Kentucky. "When you are in Atlanta again and have a little free time, I trust that I may have the pleasure of a visit with you," Dr. Caldwell said. The subject of the letter was about the number of trustees who could serve at one time, noting that the original number was four but "I am sure that Mr. Cobb has the right to amend this instrument in any way that he may see fit and to increase the size of the Board as he wishes to do so."

Then, in a May 29, 1956, letter to Dr. Elkin in Kentucky, Dr. Caldwell suggested that the next meeting of the Board had been set for Saturday, June 30, at the Capital City Club, and that 70 applications for scholarship grants had been received. Invitations were sent from Dr. Elkin to Mr. Cobb, Mr. Chandler, Dr. Kennedy, Mr. Combs, and Mr. J. B. Ritchner, Trust Officer of Trust Company of Georgia. Elkin and Caldwell, of course, completed the six-member Board.

On July 15, Dr. Elkin wrote to Carroll McMahon, who had taken over duties of Secretary from Miss Merchant earlier in the year. "I thought we had a fine meeting due to you and Dr. Caldwell," he wrote. "The next two days were somewhat hectic trying to keep Ty in shape...I ran second."

Ty Cobb also responded in a July 26, 1956, letter to Miss McMahon. Among other things, he said: "think we have a fine organization Board, etc., that includes you. I have an unusual regard for Dr. Caldwell with his interest and dignity." (*See letter on pages 71-73 in Chapter 3 - The Fund.*)

A date for the 1957 annual meeting of the Foundation turned out to be difficult to schedule, due primarily to various travel arrangements of Board members. For example: Ty Cobb was in the process of

Cobb and sportswriter O.B. Keeler at Waynesboro, Georgia, in 1925.

moving from Menlo Park, California, to Cornelia, Georgia; now living in Kentucky, Dr. Elkin could not return during July; Happy Chandler was in the middle of his second term as governor of Kentucky and was out of the country until September; and Dr. Kennedy had health and scheduling problems from his Michigan home.

Finally, the Board members who could attend – Elkin, Caldwell, Combs, and perhaps Cobb (although the records are not clear) – met on August 21, 1957, in the State Office Building in Atlanta, handing out 29 scholarships totaling $11,900, new records for the Foundation.

More troubles followed in setting an annual meeting for 1958. Ty Cobb, it seems, was "out of pocket" and had not been writing his usual long letters to Dr. Elkin and Dr. Caldwell. He had been traveling back and forth from Georgia to California, and could not be contacted for a possible meeting.

A meeting was finally set for July 31, 1958, with Elkin, Caldwell, Cobb, and Combs agreeing to make the trip to Atlanta.

As it turned out, it was a significant meeting in the history of the Foundation, for it would be the last for Dr. Elkin – he passed away just over three months later, on November 3, 1958, apparently after a long illness. In a May 25, 1958, letter from Dr. Elkin to Dr. Caldwell, the chairman wrote: "I have been ill and in the hospital or would have written you sooner."

The selection process was not completed at the July meeting, so members of the board were mailed a list of students to be considered. Awards in the amount of $12,300 were eventually made to 32 students, 12 renewals and 20 new.

Membership on the board had remained constant from late 1955 until the death of Dr. Elkin in November 1958. Dr. Caldwell, the remaining "original member" of the board, was named Chairman following Dr. Elkin's death, and his secretary, Miss McMahon, remained in place as secretary to the board.

The 1959 annual meeting was held on July 16 with Caldwell, Cobb, and Kennedy attending. Earle Combs had sent his regrets and Governor Chandler, now in the last year of his second term as governor of Kentucky, sent a note that he was "hopeful that my schedule will permit me to be with you." There is no documentation available that he was or was not able to attend.

Dr. Kennedy, who had not attended for a number of years, was coaxed into attending by Cobb, who had invited him to go with the baseball great to the annual Hall of Fame meeting in Cooperstown, New York, on July 22 and 23. Kennedy's travel plans to Cooperstown didn't work out, but Cobb did take Dr. Caldwell to the annual celebration. "My trip to Cooperstown was a delightful and interesting experience," Dr. Caldwell wrote in an August 5, 1959, letter to Dr. Kennedy. "I gained a new appreciation of the position that Mr. Cobb occupies in the world of baseball."

Cobb had flown from New York to Detroit after the

Hall of Fame ceremony for a visit with Dr. Kennedy and other friends from his Detroit playing days. "Ty came to Detroit for three or four days after leaving Cooperstown, but it was not possible for me to spend a great deal of time with him because of surgical problems that I became involved in and because of a Regents Meeting in Ann Arbor," Dr. Kennedy wrote in a follow-up letter to Dr. Caldwell.

Governor Chandler resigned from the board sometime between late 1959 and early 1960, creating another vacancy (along with Dr. Elkin's loss). Prior to that, in July 1959, two new members were invited – Dr. H. Prentice "Dean" Miller, who had worked with Dr. Elkin at Emory University, and Dr. Merritt E. Hoag, president of North Georgia College in Dahlonega, Georgia.

Dean Miller apparently had been involved with the Foundation almost from the very outset, although not as an official member of the board. In the Emory University news release naming the second set of scholarship winners in 1955, it was noted that "Dean Prentice Miller of Emory University's Lower Division and Mr. J. B. Richner of the Trust Department of Trust Company of Georgia" also attended the meeting on July 21, 1955, in addition to the Trustees, Dr. Elkin, Mrs. Cobb, Dr. Caldwell, and Gov. Chandler.

Dr. Miller served as Dean of the freshman and sophomore classes and was the first person to be named Dean of Alumni at Emory University. Dr. Hoag was well known in educational circles, having served as president of the Georgia Association of Colleges during the 1956-57 academic year.

Now living in Glenbrook, Nevada, or Menlo Park, California (it was hard to tell from his letters), Cobb made plans in early June to attend the 1960 annual meeting of the board. In a June 14, 1960, letter he wrote: "I have two meetings, both a must, Royston Cobb Memorial Hospital and Educational Foundation, Atlanta. Am trying to work in to attend baseball's Hall of Fame meeting, Cooperstown, N.Y. on June 27th to clean up my plans to follow in the east." He asked for a June 20-25 or July 1-2 meeting.

It isn't clear when the meeting was actually held, or who attended, but the 1960 meeting of the board provided a record number of 37 scholarships for Georgia students – 12 renewals and 25 new awards. Members of

the board were Dr. Caldwell as Chairman, Cobb, Dr. Kennedy, Dean Miller, Dr. Hoag, and Mr. Combs.

Yet another change was soon in store for the board. In an August 9, 1960, letter to Dr. Caldwell, Earle Combs tendered his resignation. "I have enjoyed my work with the Foundation and the association, but the last two meetings it has been impossible for me to attend," Combs said. "I recall that a resolution was passed whereby any Trustee missing two years in a row would be automatically relieved."

"I am also of the opinion that inasmuch as the Cobb Foundation is for Georgia students that the Trustees should be composed of Georgia men as they, in my opinion, would be in a better position to pass on each student," the baseball great from Kentucky continued. Combs had taken a new job as district manager for an insurance company and didn't feel he had the time for outside interests.

Thus, the Kentucky connection – Dr. Elkin, Dr. Rankin, Gov. Chandler, and now Mr. Combs – was history for the Ty Cobb Educational Foundation.

Late in 1960 and early 1961, Ty Cobb was in failing health and apparently traveled a lot between Atlanta, Royston, Menlo Park, California, Glenbrook (Lake Tahoe), Nevada, and Phoenix, Arizona.

In a January 19, 1961, letter from Dean Miller to Cobb, the newest Foundation Trustee related: "It was indeed a pleasure and a delight to see you in the Emory Hospital just before you were being dismissed as a patient." Apparently, during their meeting, Cobb had suggested Mr. Claude Purcell as a possible member of the board. "I am sure that the other Trustees of the Cobb Foundation will be interested in Mr. Claude Purcell," Miller wrote. "I have known Mr. Purcell for years, and he has my unqualified respect."

Later in the letter, he noted that Mr. Purcell might not have the time to serve. "I do know there are endless nightmares and vicious cross currents involved in public education in Georgia, and as Superintendent of Schools, his responsibility and problems are endless," he said.

"Needless to say, the state of Georgia is in the greatest uproar of my lifetime," Miller wrote, "and in various ways Chancellor Caldwell and Mr. Purcell are in the middle of it. As soon as the Legislature has settled all the educational matters for the time being, at least, and have adjourned, I shall take up the matter at length with Chancellor Caldwell and the other Trustees. I am confident that they will be very much interested in his appointment."

Also in the letter he referred to the Supreme Court's decision of 1954 and of the results and repercussions of that decision on education ranks.

Additional information on the possible appointment of Mr. Purcell is not noted in the files, but the Superintendent was never named to the board.

In a short note to Miss McMahon from Cornelia, Georgia, on February 25, 1961, Cobb agreed to drop a student from the program and reported "I am not exactly enjoying your Georgia weather." He said he was leaving around the first of March for Phoenix, Arizona, "for a month or more" and gave her his address. Then, he planned to be back in Menlo Park, California, in early April for two or three weeks. *(See letter on pages 102-103 in Chapter 3 - The Fund.)*

In an April 20, 1961, letter from one of his western locations, Cobb responded to information about yet another student and eluded to the upcoming annual meeting, although a date was not included. In a P.S. to his short note, Cobb wrote: "Please notify Dr. Kennedy and of course the other members of the board, to attend this coming meeting - a <u>must</u>. I have some director medallions to present. Merely state it is my particular desire that all directors be there this particular time." *(See letter on page 104 in Chapter 3 - The Fund.)*

This historic meeting was scheduled for July 14, 1961....but, Ty Cobb was not in attendance. He was seriously ill and in the hospital where he would die on July 17.

In an earlier letter (June 27, 1961), Dr. Kennedy had related to Miss McMahon that he indeed would be at the annual meeting, and addressed another subject. "It was really too bad that the Medallion arrived before Ty had planned," he wrote. "There is one redeeming feature which is that the Medallion, together with a number of photographs which Ty has given to me off and on, are now on exhibition at the Detroit Public Library with an Old Timers group of pictures of Baseball Celebrities going back to 1885. This town is all excited about the present Tigers and the Old Timers Exhibit is attracting a lot of attention."

Later in the letter he noted that "I have written to Ty several times lately but either my letters have gone astray or he has not been in the mood to answer – poor

Cobb demonstrating his bunting technique

fellow. I feel sorry for him." (*See letter on page 118.*)

Then, in a July 24, 1961, letter from Detroit, Dr. Kennedy talked about his last visit with Ty Cobb. "I was so glad that it was possible for me to go to Atlanta to attend the Cobb Educational Foundation meeting," he wrote. "I am sure that you and the rest of the good folks associated with that project are accomplishing much in a fine field. One cannot read the records of the various applicants without being sure that a lot of good youngsters that otherwise would not have the opportunity to complete a college education are being given aid which would not otherwise be available."

"Another reason that I was particularly glad to have gone to Atlanta ten days ago was that I had an opportunity to visit with Mrs. Cobb and her family and on Saturday afternoon, had a talk with Ty for ten or fifteen minutes during his last lucid interval," Dr. Kennedy continued. "I left the family in a nearby reception room to go upstairs to visit Ty, found that he knew me, talked with him for a few moments and then hurried downstairs to advise the family to hurry to see him while he was still clear. It is my understanding that they all visited with him for a short time before he lapsed once more into irrationality from which he never again recovered."

Dr. Kennedy had high praise for Ty Cobb. "Many experiences that I had with him during his tumultuous life will never be forgotten," he said. "He certainly was a stormy petrel who was always seeking something which he never quite attained. I was constantly being impressed with the breadth of his knowledge, the intensity of his efforts to attain his objective as well as the religious streak which governed many of his actions, despite the fact that side of his nature was usually suppressed. Mechanically, he was the greatest baseball player who ever lived, or ever will in my judgment, but in addition to that, he had a mentality and a drive which would have made him an outstanding success in any profession or business which he might have undertaken. It was a great experience to have known him."

The July 14, 1961, annual meeting must have been difficult for all Trustees, but nonetheless, they provided a record number of 46 scholarships for students to attend classes during the 1961-62 year, a total expense of $19,000.

Cobb would have been proud!

And, even in death, Ty Cobb was adding to his educational dream. In lieu of flowers, the family requested that donations be made to the Cobb Educational Foundation, and a series of monetary gifts from around the country began almost immediately. In addition, although it would take a number of years to complete, Cobb's final will and testament provided for a fourth of his total holdings to go to the Foundation.

With the resignation of Mr. Combs in 1960 and death of Ty Cobb in 1961, the Board of Trustees was down to four members – Chairman Caldwell, Dr. Kennedy, Dr. Miller, and Dr. Hoag. And, it would remain that way until early 1963.

"For some time I have been thinking that I should direct this letter to you regretfully tendering my resignation as a member of the Ty Cobb Foundation," wrote Dr. Kennedy in a February 18, 1963, letter to Dr. Caldwell. Noting that he had reached his 75th birthday and was suffering from the "slings and arrows of advancing years," the Detroit doctor suggested that "it would be wise if you and the other members of the Foundation would select a younger man than I to carry on."

"My fondest wish is that the Ty Cobb Fund will continue to carry out the wonderful work which it has started for a great many years to come," he added.

In his response on behalf of the board, Dr. Caldwell expressed thanks to Dr. Kennedy "for the magnificent services that you rendered as a charter member of the Board." (It should be pointed out here that Dr. Kennedy was not a charter member, having joined the board along with Cobb in early 1955.)

"Mr. Ty Cobb regarded you as one of his dearest friends and he had complete confidence in your ability and judgment," he continued. "You helped the Board through its difficult first years and you won the lasting gratitude of Mr. Cobb and his friends."

The three-member board met for its annual meeting in Atlanta on July 1-2, 1963, and elected Dr. S. Walter Martin, vice chancellor of the University System of Georgia, to succeed Dr. Kennedy. Like Dr. Hoag, Dr. Martin was a past president of the Georgia Association of Colleges (1961-62 while serving as president of Emory University) and was well known around the state. He had been named vice chancellor in 1962.

Additional members were not named for the next 14 years, although changes on the board were taking place. Dean Miller was named the board's first vice chairman in January 1966, taking on more responsibilities as head of the organization. And, 11 years later, in January 1977, Dr. Caldwell was named chairman emeritus and Dean Miller became the third chairman of the board for the fledging Foundation.

Also in January 1977, Dr. Harry S. Downs, president of Clayton Junior College in Morrow, Georgia, became the first new appointment to the board since 1963.

Dr. Caldwell died on April 15, 1977, ending an era with the Ty Cobb Foundation that started in 1953. Before his death, he was the last remaining member of the original Board of Trustees.

Dean Miller stepped down as chairman of the board during 1982-83 year, but remained active on the Foundation until his death in November 1985. He officially completed 26 years on the Cobb Foundation Board of Trustees, but as before mentioned, had been associated with the Fund long before his 1959 appointment. In addition to his service with Emory University and the Cobb Foundation, Miller also served as secretary–treasurer for the Georgia Association of Colleges for 26 years (1958-1984), serving far beyond his retirement from professional education.

Dr. Downs became the fourth chairman of the board when Dr. Miller withdrew, and remained in the position more than 20 years later as the Foundation celebrated its 50th anniversary. His long educational career included service as vice chancellor of the University System of Georgia, president of Clayton Junior College/Clayton State College for 25 years, and interim chancellor of the University System of Georgia

for six months. In 1994, after stepping down as the founding president of Clayton State, he was named to serve as interim chancellor until a permanent appointment could be made to succeed Chancellor H. Dean Propst. Among his many appointments, Dr. Downs also served as president of the Georgia Association of Colleges (1990-91).

Dr. Hoag, retired by then as president of North Georgia College, resigned as an active board member in January 1984 and was named board member emeritus. He continued to meet with the board on a limited basis until his death in November 1994, more than 10 years later. Appointed to the board in late 1959, Dr. Hoag had been associated with the Foundation for 35 years at the time of his death and was the last remaining member who had actually served at the same time with Ty Cobb.

Following a distinguished career in the military service, Dr. Hoag was named president of North Georgia College. Then, after retiring from North Georgia, he served as mayor and in other leadership capacities for the city of Young Harris, Georgia.

Cobb in 1906, his first full season in the American League.

Dr. Derrell Roberts, president of Dalton Junior College (Dalton, Georgia), was appointed to replace Dr. Hoag during 1984-85 year.

Dr. Walter Y. Murphy, president of LaGrange College (LaGrange, Georgia), was appointed to the board in January 1987.

Dr. Martin, retired at this time as president of Valdosta State College, resigned from active membership on the board in January 1998. He was named board member emeritus and continued to serve on a limited capacity until his death in June 2000.

Appointed to the board in 1963, Dr. Martin's official service to the Foundation was a month short of 37 years. Unofficially, however, it was much longer than that. Having worked as vice chancellor under Dr. Caldwell, he was very familiar with the Foundation for a number of years before being appointed.

Like Dr. Hoag, who had passed away six years earlier, Dr. Martin also had dealings with Ty Cobb, although he did not officially join the board until two years after Cobb's death.

During his educational career, Dr. Martin had served in a number of administrative positions at the University of Georgia, including dean of the College of Arts and Sciences from 1949-57. He served as president of Emory University from 1957-62, and as vice chancellor with the University System of Georgia from 1961-66. When Dr. Caldwell retired on July 1, 1964, Dr. Martin temporarily replaced him as chancellor until the new chancellor, George L. Simpson, was elected. Finally, Dr. Martin served as president of Valdosta State College, now Valdosta State University, from 1966-78.

Dr. Francis J. Tedesco, president of the Medical College of Georgia, replaced Dr. Martin on the board in January 1998.

Dr. Roberts, then retired as president of Dalton Junior College, died rather unexpectedly in January 2002. Dr. Roberts capped a long career in education by serving as president of Dalton Junior/Dalton State College between 1970 and 1994, and was named president emeritus upon his retirement. In 1997, the Board of Regents of the University System of Georgia honored the historian educator by naming "The Derrell C. Roberts Library" at Dalton State College in honor of his outstanding service.

Still active until his death, Dr. Roberts had served the Foundation and the students of Georgia for 18 years.

The Foundation headed into its second 50 years at the start of the 2004 year with four members on the board. Dr. Downs, now president emeritus of Clayton College and State University (formerly Clayton Junior/Clayton State College), continued to serve as chairman of the board. In his 27th year as a board mem-

Cobb with Hughey Jennings as Cobb becomes Tigers manager 1921.

ber, Downs had been chairman since 1982.

Dr. Murphy, now president emeritus of LaGrange College, continued to serve with 17 years on the board. He served as president of LaGrange College, the oldest private college in Georgia (founded in 1831 and affiliated with The United Methodist Church) from 1980-96. In addition to his educational service, Dr. Murphy is a past district governor for Rotary International.

Dr. Tedesco, now president emeritus of the Medical College of Georgia (MCG), continued to serve with six years on the board. He graduated from St. Louis University School of Medicine in 1969 and taught at the University of Pennsylvania, Washington University School of Medicine, and the University of Miami School of Medicine before joining MCG faculty in 1978 as an associate professor of medicine and chief of

the Section of Gastroenterology. He was promoted to professor in 1981, and the Board of Regents inaugurated Dr. Tedesco as the sixth president of MCG on July 1, 1988. He retired in 2001 and was named president emeritus.

Dr. Edward D. Jackson, Jr., president of South Georgia College, became the newest member of the board upon his appointment in January 2004. Formerly the dean of instruction at Tallahassee Community College, Dr. Jackson came to Georgia in February 1983 as president of the public associate degree granting college in Douglas, Georgia. "I look forward to helping worthy young men and women achieve their educational goals through the support provided by the Ty Cobb Educational Foundation," he said following his appointment to the board. Like other members of the board, he also has served as president of the Georgia Association of Colleges (1992-93).

THE SCHOLARSHIP BOARD – *Taking a pause at the 1993 annual meeting of the Board of Trustees, held at on the Morrow, Georgia, campus of Clayton Junior College were (from left), Dr. Derrell C. Roberts, Dr. S. Walter Martin, Dr. Merritt E. Hoag (Emeritus member), Dr. Walter Y. Murphy, and Dr. Harry S. Downs. Dr. Hoag died the following year (November 1994), Dr. Martin died in June 2000, and Dr. Roberts died unexpectedly in January 2002. Dr. Murphy and Dr. Downs remained on the Board at the start of 2004.*

TRUSTEES OF THE TY COBB EDUCATIONAL FOUNDATION – 1953-2004

CHARLES S. KENNEDY, M. D.
ELMER B. MILLER, M. D.
DONALD C. McLEAN, M. D.
210 PROFESSIONAL BUILDING
WOODWARD AT PETERBORO
DETROIT 1

Telephone
TEmple 1-2213
TEmple 1-6610

June 27, 1961

Miss Carroll McMahon
244 Washington St. S.W.
Atlanta 3, Georgia

Dear Miss McMahon:

I have been expecting the letter which arrived from
you yesterday for sometime. I shall set aside both
July 13th and 14th and be on hand on either date which
you decide upon, but hope that you will let me know soon
so that I can make reservations to leave Detroit the afternoon of the day before the meeting. I shall also appreciate it if you will make a reservation for an airconditioned
room for me in any hotel which you think desirable.

It was really too bad that the Medallion arrived before Ty had planned. There is one redeeming feature which
is that the Medallion together with a number of photographs
which Ty has given to me off and on are now on exhibition
at the Detroit Public Library with an Old Timers group of
pictures of Baseball Celebrities going back to 1885. This
town is all excited about the present Tigers and the Old
Timers Exhibit is attracting a lot of attention.

I have written to Ty several times lately but either
my letters have gone astray or he has not been in the mood
to answer--poor fellow I feel sorry for him.

Please let me know as soon as you have definitely
decided on the date for the Foundation Meeting since one
or the other of my associates will be away on vacation
during July and August and I would like to be able to
plan the future definitely as soon as possible.

With every good wish all around,

Sincerely yours,

Charles S. Kennedy, M.D.

CSK/mo

118

CHAPTER FIVE

Secretaries to the Board

"My desire is whatever you do or is to be done, I would like it to take a very minimum of your time. Have a setup where it will work automatically, some stenographer or secretary to handle the details."

– December 9, 1953, letter from Ty Cobb to Dr. Daniel C. Elkin who would Chair the Ty Cobb Educational Fund

"Letters of inquiry have been of little concern so far and my own secretarial staff has been glad to handle it. I think sometime in the future, however, it would be well to secure the part-time services of a secretary who could handle this work after hours or on off days, possibly on an hourly basis."

– December 16, 1953, letter from Dr. Daniel C. Elkin to Ty Cobb

ALICE MERCHANT (1953-1956)

Miss Alice Merchant, secretary to Daniel C. Elkin, M.D., Department of Surgery, Emory University Hospital, served as the first secretary to the Ty Cobb Educational Foundation, starting in late 1953 and leaving the position in early 1956.

A natural selection, since Dr. Elkin was the first Chairman of the Scholarship Board, correspondence from Miss Merchant can be found as far back as December 1953 when the Foundation (of Fund as it was

sometimes called) was just getting off the ground.

And, since Dr. Elkin obviously was a very busy man, the contributions of Miss Merchant were instrumental in the start-up of the Foundation. In fact, from the files of the Foundation, it appears that she managed most of the activities of the Scholarship Board such as communications with student applicants, college and university financial aid directors, Ty Cobb and other Trustees, and the news media. In addition, she also set up meeting places for the Board.

In an August 20, 1954, letter to Mr. and Mrs. Ty Cobb, Miss Merchant provided information about the Board's initial scholarships made the previous month and forwarded them copies of various news releases.

"I was most appreciative of your generous check to me for the little I have done in connection with the work of the Cobb Educational Foundation," she said in her letter to the Cobbs. "I have counted it a real privilege to have participated in the carrying out of Mr. Cobb's wonderful gift to these young students. The personal contact with several of them has been heartwarming because they have all been such worthwhile young people and are sincerely appreciative of the interest Mr. Cobb has shown in their welfare."

Records aren't clear exactly when Dr. Elkin retired from Emory University, but it appears that it happened sometime during 1955, the second year of the Foundation. Upon (or before) his retirement, Dr. Elkin moved back to Lancaster, Kentucky, and was only a frequent visitor to Atlanta, although he retained the position as chairman of the Scholarship Board.

Miss Merchant continued her duties after Dr. Elkin had left, but eventually decided to return to school and complete a law degree. So, near the end of 1955, she began making preparations for a change for the Foundation.

In a September 2, 1955, letter to Mr. Cobb, she wrote: "It is too bad that you are not in my position here because I get to talk with them (the students) when they come through town and see them when they come by the office seeking to speak with Dr. Elkin. It will be interesting through the years to see how wonderfully these young people will turn out, and it must be a great satisfaction to you to realize the part you are playing in making their lives so successful and happy."

Later in that same letter, she wrote of missing her former boss. "Dr. Elkin has talked with me almost every day recently as he has a friend from Lancaster who has been our patient here," she said. "We miss him here because he is such a cute person, and I know how very much he thinks of you. He mentions you in almost every letter and has told me of the fine letters you have received from our scholars."

In another letter written just five days later (September 7), Miss Merchant said: "We are looking for Dr. Elkin to come back to Atlanta some time this fall on a quick business trip and only wish that you could come back to join him."

Then, she talked of a change that would include the secretary to Dr. Harmon W. Caldwell, chancellor of the University System of Georgia and an original board member of the Foundation.

"I have not yet had a chance to visit with Dr. Caldwell's secretary to give her some details of the work of the Cobb Foundation," she started. "She has tentatively indicated that she will be willing to take over when I leave the first of the year. Perhaps my hesitancy in speaking with her likes almost in the fact that I hate so badly to turn the job over to anyone. It has been a source of real pleasure to me, and I almost wonder at times if it might not be better for me to make a legal connection in Atlanta in order to stick with the Cobb Foundation!

"Please rest assured, however, that I shall see that the affairs of the Foundation are placed in competent hands before I do leave," Miss Merchant continued. "I am still grateful for the kind sentiments you have always expressed to me about the small part I have played in this wonderful undertaking, and I assure you that your confidence in me has meant a great deal."

Then, on January 10, 1956, Miss Merchant wrote to Miss Carroll McMahon at the Board of Regents. "It is wonderful that you are now in a position to take over the Cobb files for me after February 15th," she said. "I will certainly contact you the last of this month and arrange for you to come over for supper with me and a brief survey of the situation. I do promise you that you will find the task a very pleasant one. I feel so good about being able to turn the matter over to your capable handling."

CARROLL McMAHON (1956-1980)

And so, the stage was set. Miss Merchant enrolled at the University of Alabama to complete her law degree. "Even the heavens cried when you left!" wrote Miss McMahon in a February 20, 1956, letter to Miss Merchant. Then, she presented a long list of questions for the Foundation's inaugural secretary to answer.

In her reply almost a month later, Miss Merchant answered each question in a long and detailed manner. Then, she talked about her plans. "I am quite pleasantly situated back here at the University and am looking forward to being a bona fide lawyer within a matter of weeks now," she said. "I shall probably settle in Montgomery, Alabama, although it is hard to resist the temptation of returning to Atlanta on a permanent basis."

One of the questions pertained to sending copies of letters to Board members. "Do not bother about sending Dr. Elkin any copies as he knows that you are taking care of the affairs of the Foundation," she said. "Speaking quite frankly, Dr. Caldwell was the only other Trustee bearing any of the responsibility for the work of the Foundation. Gov. Chandler and Mr. Combs were mere figureheads and didn't want to be concerned, so I think it is quite unnecessary to advise them about any of the proceedings other than the most formal aspects like the annual meeting, etc. (she was referring to Kentucky Governor Albert B.

"Happy" Chandler and Mr. Earle Combs of Richmond, Kentucky, a former major leaguer and friend of Mr. Cobb).

"Always conserve your time and energy when you can because this can develop into a large undertaking and full-time responsibility if you do not watch it," she concluded.

So, the change was made. Carroll McMahon began her duties in early 1956, serving with a Board that included Ty Cobb, Dr. Elkin, Dr. Caldwell, Gov. Chandler, Mr. Combs, and Dr. Charles S. Kennedy, a Detroit physician.

In a letter dated July 26, 1956, after her first meeting with the Board, Miss McMahon received a letter from Ty Cobb. He thanked her for the information about that meeting, held on June 30 at the Capital City Club in Atlanta. "You have sent me something that I have for many months wanted, that is to see the <u>pictures</u> of the boys and girls, also their records and what those in their interest for each thought of their qualifications. You have pleased me much." *(See letter on pages 71-73 in Chapter 3 - The Fund.)*

"Think we have a fine organization board, etc. that also means you," Cobb continued later in the 3-page letter. "I have an unusual regard for Dr. Caldwell with his interest and dignity."

Carroll McMahon held the duties for over 25 years, dealing with many changes in the Board, including the chairman's position. Dr. Elkin was still chairman when she started, followed by Dr. Caldwell (1959) and then Dr. H. Prentice "Dean" Miller of Emory University (1977). Members joining the board during that stretch included Dr. Miller (1959); Dr. Merritt B. Hoag, president of North Georgia College (1959); Dr. Walter S. Martin, vice chancellor of the University System of Georgia (1963); and Dr. Harry S. Downs, president of Clayton Junior College (1977).

During that time period, Dr. Elkin died (1958), Gov. Chandler resigned (1960), Ty Cobb died (1961), Mr. Combs resigned (1960), Dr. Kennedy resigned (1963), and Dr. Caldwell died (1977).

As secretary, Miss McMahon saw awards vault from $8,900 during her first year in 1956 to $163,200 during her last year of service in 1980.

Official files of the Foundation indicate that Miss McMahon had a difficult time in scheduling annual meetings of the Board, especially during the 1950s when so many of the members were from out of state (including Ty Cobb). Communications with all Board members flew back and forth for weeks while she and Dr. Caldwell worked to hold meetings in time to notify students prior to the beginning of fall semester or quarter classes. Ty Cobb always seemed to have a conflict with attending the Foundation's annual meeting and also the annual Hall of Fame meeting in Cooperstown, New York. *(See numerous letters in Chapter 3 - The Fund.)*

DAN HARDAGE - DIANNE JORDAN (1981)

Mr. Jack D. "Dan" Hardage, a member of the faculty at Clayton Junior College (CJC), was named secretary to the Foundation in January 1981, but his tenure was cut short by his untimely death later that year. Dianne Jordan, secretary to Dr. Downs at CJC, took over the duties on a temporary basis for the rest of 1981.

ROSIE ATKINS (1982-2003)

Mrs. Rosie C. Atkins, a self-employed computer technician from Clayton County, became secretary to the Board in January 1982, beginning a tenure that lasted for the next 22 years and carrying the Foundation into its 50th year of existence.

Members of the Board in 1982 were Dr. Miller as chairman, Dr. Downs, Dr. Martin and Dr. Hoag. Dr. Downs was appointed chairman during that year as the Board once again began to change. Dr. Hoag resigned as an active member and took up emeritus status in early 1984, but continued to meet with the board for the next 10 years.

Dr. Derrell C. Roberts, president of Dalton Junior College, was named to the board in 1984 as a replacement for Dr. Hoag.

Dean Miller passed away in November 1985, and Dr. Walter Y. Murphy, president of LaGrange College, was appointed to the board in 1987.

Changes to the board were slow during the next few years until Dr. Hoag died in November 1994. Dr. Francis J. Tedesco, president of the Medical College of Georgia, was appointed to the board in January 1998. Dr. Martin took emeritus status in early 1998 and passed away in June 2000. Dr. Roberts died unexpectedly in January 2002.

As with previous secretaries, Mrs. Atkins dealt with

students, financial aid directors at various colleges and universities, and officers at Trust Company Bank, in addition to scheduling meetings and corresponding with members of the board.

In the 22 years Mrs. Atkins served as secretary, she managed almost $8 million in funds awarded to Georgia students by the Board – a grand total of $7,803,083.00. A total of 4,262 scholarships were handed out during that period, including new and renewal awards.

During her first year, the Board awarded a then-record number of 253 students a total of $190,925.00 also a record at that point. The highest total awarded during the 22-year span was 274 students for the 2001-02 year, and total of $644,334.00 awarded that year also ranks as the highest ever provided for students during a single year. The Board topped the half million dollar mark ($525,668.00) for the first time during the 1997-98 year.

In addition to dealing with the vast number of students receiving awards, the secretary also corresponded and kept files for several hundred additional students (sometimes close to 2,000) each year.

CHERYL O'KEEFE (2004-2005)

Three significant changes took place as the Ty Cobb Educational Foundation entered its second 50 years of existence at the start of the 2004 year:

– The home office of the Foundation has been moved from Forest Park to Augusta;

– Cheryl O'Keeffe was named as the fund's secretary; and,

– Dr. Edward D. Jackson, Jr., president of South Georgia College in Douglas, was appointed to the scholarship board.

The office of the scholarship foundation had moved from its original location in Atlanta to Forest Park in 1981. The new location is on the campus of the Medical College of Georgia.

O'Keeffe, who holds both a bachelor's degree in journalism (cum laude, 1966) and a master's degree (1968) from the University of Georgia, served as director of Student Financial Aid at the Medical College of Georgia from 1975 through 1992. Prior to that, from 1969 through 1974, she held the position as director of Student Financial Aid and Career Planning and Placement at Augusta College.

Dr. Jackson joined three other Georgia educators on the prestigious board, including Dr. Downs of Conyers, president emeritus at Clayton College and State University who continues to serve as chairman; Dr. Murphy of LaGrange, president emeritus of LaGrange College; and Dr. Tedesco of Augusta, president emeritus of the Medical College of Georgia.

A FOOTNOTE ABOUT THE MANY PROBLEMS OF SECRETARIES

Dealing with students hasn't always been an easy procedure for past secretaries of the Ty Cobb Educational Foundation.

Take for example the announcement of the Foundation's first six scholarship recipients in 1954. In a letter to Mr. and Mrs. Ty Cobb, Alice Merchant, who was the first secretary to the Foundation, wrote that checks had been sent to the schools involved to cover the six scholarships.

"Upon forwarding the $500 check to Mercer University for one of our students, we were informed that he had been admitted to the University of Georgia School of Medicine and would be continuing his education there this fall," she wrote. "As the award had already been made to the student, request was made that check for this grant be reissued and forwarded to the University of Georgia."

This process, or one like it, has been repeated for 50 years.

CHAPTER SIX

Ty Cobb and Baseball

Many great players have surfaced on the diamond, but none out-hit, out-played, or out-hustled the man they called "The Georgia Peach."

– From the official web site of Ty Cobb

This book is not about Ty Cobb, the baseball great. It's about the educational foundation established late in the life of Ty Cobb. However, the success of Ty Cobb on the baseball field is, in fact, the reason that the educational foundation ever existed. Without the great wealth accumulated by the baseball great as a player, there never would have been money available to consider such an endeavor.

Yes, Ty Cobb probably could have been very successful in the business world and the money could have come from other means. In fact, because of his personal drive, and his temperament to win at all costs, there's every reason to believe he would have been successful in whatever field he entered. After all, he was quoted as saying: "I've got to be first all the time – in everything."

But, baseball is what he chose...and baseball paid him big dividends.

When Ty Cobb retired in 1928, his earnings on the baseball field and his wise investments off the field made him very wealthy and probably baseball's first millionaire. His annual haggles with the Detroit Tiger execu-

tives before signing contracts are well documented, as are his investments, mostly with General Motors and Coca-Cola. Although Ty Cobb's top annual salary as a baseball player was less than $40,000, his shrewd investments made him a financial success at an early age.

The story of Ty Cobb's baseball career is well documented in numerous books and major league baseball files. So, we'll leave the heavy details to those publications while providing the highlights in this publication, which is about one of his greatest rewards – the Ty Cobb Educational Foundation.

During 24 seasons, 22 with the Detroit Tigers and 2 with the Philadelphia Athletics, Cobb compiled a .367 batting average, the highest in the history of the game. He retired as the leader in runs scored with 2,245, and was the all-time hit leader until the mid-1980s when Pete Rose claimed the record.

In 1936, Ty Cobb became the first inductee of baseball's Hall of Fame, earning 222 out of a possible 226 votes cast by members of the Base Ball Writers Association of America (BBWAA). To qualify for the first group of inductees, a player had to receive 75 percent of the votes and Cobb was only four shy of unanimity. The great Babe Ruth, who had just retired the year before, and Honus Wagner were tied for second with 215 votes, with Christy Mathewson (205) and Walter Johnson (189) being the only other players selected. This Hall of Fame vote, it was well known, was one of the proudest moments in Cobb's baseball career.

Just how big was the vote for Ty Cobb in that very first poll? Well, Major League Baseball reported in 1964 that in the 29 years of voting, no player had received a unanimous vote from the writers. And, the nearest approach to unanimity came with Cobb's 222 out of 226 votes, more than 98 percent. Ruth and Wagner each received 95 percent of the vote.

It is unlikely that anyone can beat Cobb's .367 lifetime batting average. In his 24 seasons of playing baseball he topped the .300 barrier 23 times. Cobb's first great season came in 1907, his third season in the majors, and the Tigers rode that success all the way to the World Series. The centerfielder's batting average was .350 and was the first of nine consecutive batting titles in the American League (AL).

Cobb looked for every possible way to win, using his great speed and precision hitting as the best weapons available in the dead-ball, strong-pitching era. He studied pitchers and took advantage of their weaknesses.

His best years were 1911, when he led the league in every major offensive category but homers and batted a career high .420, and in 1915 when he stole 96 bases.

The 1911 season was his seventh with the Tigers. That year, he set career highs in runs (147), hits (248), doubles (47), triples (24), RBI (127), average (.420), and slugging percentage (.621). He led the AL in each category, as well as with 83 stolen bases (second only to his 1915 total). He missed the Triple Crown by three homers as Frank "Home Run" Baker led with 11.

He also set a then AL record with a 40-game hitting streak, which helped him edge Shoeless Joe Jackson for the batting title. Over the course of the season Cobb

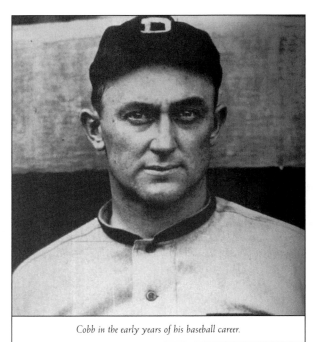

Cobb in the early years of his baseball career.

struck out swinging just two times. The numbers overshadowed Cobb's combative personality and won him the first ever MVP, then called the Chalmers Award. Auto dealer Hugh Chalmers had presented Cobb with a Chalmers "30" for winning the 1910 batting title, and followed that with another flashy automobile for winning the MVP in 1911.

Cobb spent a little over two years in the minor leagues before being called up at the age of 19 by the Tigers late in the 1905 season. He had a .326 batting average in 103 games for Augusta in the Sally League before hitting only .240 in 41 games with Detroit after his August 30 call-up. In the majors to stay, Cobb hit .320 in 1906 and the best hitter of his era, if not of all time, was off and running.

He insisted that he was not a super athlete, but rather had a great desire to win. His .367 career batting average, however, easily qualified him as a "super athlete" that baseball would long remember.

Cobb might be remembered best for his intimidating and harsh playing style. He was never afraid to go to extremes to win a game, taking the pain as well as handing it out. He overlooked no opportunity to gain an edge over his opponents, most of whom admired his drive to succeed.

Cobb was also the greatest of his generation on the base paths. Using an aggressive, unconventional fall-away slide, Cobb stole a league-leading 49 bases in 1909, the first of his six base-stealing crowns. He stole his personal high, a then-record 96, in 1915. Cobb's career total of 892 steals stood as the all-time mark for nearly half a century. Cobb still holds the record for most steals of home, with more than 50 (the exact total is in dispute). On four occasions, he stole second, third, and home in the same inning, also a record.

"Rarely should a base runner risk a steal when the game is in balance. It's to be used when you can afford to fail," Cobb said. "Most of all I was saddling that team with a psychological burden so that they would be muttering, Cobb is crazy. He'll run anytime and in any situation. It would help give them the jitters and they'd concentrate so much on me they were not paying any attention to the business at hand. My failures rarely were complete failures. They were more like future investments."

Check out some of these outstanding accomplishments.

TYRUS RAYMOND COBB
"THE GEORGIA PEACH"

– was considered the best hitter of his era, if not all time;
– finished with a career batting average of .367;
– batted under .320 only once in his career;
– batted over .400 three times, including his best at .420;
– was the youngest American League player to reach 1,000 hits (age 24);

– won 12 batting titles, including nine in a row from 1907 through 1915;
– set the record for all-time stolen bases with 892 (broken in 1990);
– stole home a record 50 times (stealing home is a rare feat these days);
– set the record in career hits with 4,191 (broken in 1985);
– scored 100 runs 11 times in his 24-year career;
– drove in over 100 runs seven times in his career;
– led the American League in runs five times and in hits eight times;
– was a player–manager for the Tigers between 1921 and 1926.

"Baseball is a red-blooded sport for a red-blooded man. It's no pink tea, and mollycoddles had better stay out. It's a struggle for supremacy, survival of the fittest."
– Ty Cobb as a player

"The great trouble with baseball today is that most of the play-

Cobb sliding safely into third at Bennett Park, Detroit, 1909.

ers are in the game for the money and that's it. Not for the love of it, the excitement of it, the thrill of it."

— **Ty Cobb as a player–manager in 1925**

TYRUS RAYMOND "TY" COBB
BASEBALL CAREER IN A NUTSHELL

Nicknames – "The Georgia Peach" or just "Peach"

Played For – Detroit Tigers (1905-1926), Philadelphia A's (1927-1928)

Cobb at Yankee Stadium 1923.

Managed – Detroit Tigers (1921-1926)

Post-Season – 1907 World Series, 1908 World Series, 1909 World Series

World Champion? – No

Honors – 1911 American League Most Valuable Player

Feats – Six times in his career, Cobb reached base and

proceeded to steal second, third and home. The first time he did it was in 1907, the final time was in 1924...On May 5, 1925, Cobb blasted three homers, a double, and two singles in one game, for a then-record 16 total bases. The next day he hit two more homers.

Top Players Of Cobb's Time – Honus Wagner, Nap Lajoie, Sam Crawford, Walter Johnson, "Shoeless" Joe Jackson, Babe Ruth, Harry Heilmann, Heinie Manush, Charlie Gehringer, Tris Speaker, Christy Mathewson, Frank "Home Run" Baker, Eddie Collins, Jimmy Foxx, Lou Gehrig, Mickey Cochrane, Lefty Grove, George Sisler, Grover Cleveland Alexander, Harold "Pie" Traynor.

Position – OF (2,934 games), 1B (14), pitcher (3), 2B (2), 3B (1). Cobb was primarily a center fielder, with the exception of the Tigers pennant years of 1907-1909.

Major League Debut – August 30, 1905

Milestones – Collected his 3,000th hit on Aug. 19, 1921; 4,000th hit on July 19, 1927

Hitting Streaks – 40 games (1911), 35 games (1917), 25 games (1906)

A Fact – Ty Cobb is one of only two people to hit a home run before his 20th birthday and after his 40th birthday (the other is Rusty Staub).

Winner or Loser? – It's well chronicled that Cobb never won a World Series, though he played in three Fall Classics, all as a young man, prior to his peak as a player. His teams were competitive however: in his 19 seasons as a regular, the teams he played on were 1542-1331, a .537 winning percentage.

Run Producer – No player in baseball history drove in more teammates than did Cobb. When you subtract home runs from RBI, you have the number of teammates batted in (TBI), Cobb leads all-time with 1,843.

Best Strengths as a Player – Base running and batting eye.

Largest Weakness as a Player – Cobb had no weakness on a ball field.

CHAPTER SEVEN

The Ty Cobb Museum

As a not-for-profit, educational institution, the Ty Cobb Museum will foster an appreciation for the life and career of Tyrus Raymond Cobb and his impact on the game of baseball by collecting, preserving, exhibiting, and interpreting artifacts related to Cobb for a local, regional, and national audience.

– Mission Statement for the Ty Cobb Museum, Royston, Georgia

The Ty Cobb Museum is located in the Joe A. Adams Professional Building of the Ty Cobb Healthcare System in Ty Cobb's hometown of Royston.

A not-for-profit educational institution, The Ty Cobb Museum was officially dedicated in July 1998 with a mission "to foster education and understanding to the broadest possible audience of the greatest baseball hitter of all time, Tyrus Raymond Cobb."

The museum fosters the education and understanding of baseball and Ty Cobb by providing art and memorabilia, film, video, books, and many other historical archives.

Professionally designed, the museum features rare photographs and artifacts, including Cobb's 1907 American League batting champion medal.

Also included is the "Cobb Theater" featuring stadium-style seating accented by a beautiful mural along with a stirring video featuring the narration of Georgia broadcasting legend Larry Munson and interviews with Atlanta Braves star Chipper Jones and ESPN baseball analyst Peter Gammons. Rare footage and still photographs bring Ty Cobb's memory to life.

Open throughout the year, with the exception of designated holidays, the Museum is located at 461 Cook Street in Royston. Hours of operation are between 9:00 A.M. and 4:00 P.M. Monday through Friday and between 10:00 A.M. to 4:00 P.M. on Saturdays.

Past donations to the Museum have provided outstanding collections and the Ty Cobb Museum Committee realizes that there are many more great stories which could be a part of its exhibition. "Gifts of objects associated with baseball's history are essential to the growth and educational potential of the Ty Cobb Museum and are actively sought by the Museum," the Museum's Committee states on its web site.

Possible contributions to the collection are constantly under review. "If you own an object that is part of our baseball history and you would be interested in sharing it with fans everywhere, then we would like to hear from you," the Committee states.

Such proposals, with documented information, should be directed to The Registrar, Ty Cobb Museum, 461 Cook Street, Royston, GA 30662-3903.

Through its mission, the Museum is committed to:

÷ Collecting Ty Cobb baseball artifacts, works of art, literature, photographs, memorabilia, and other materials related to Cobb's life.

÷ Preserving the collections by adhering to professional standards with respect to conservation and maintaining a permanent record of holdings through documentation, study, research, cataloguing, and publication.

÷ Exhibiting material in permanent gallery space located within the Ty Cobb Museum, organizing on-site changing exhibitions on various themes, with works from the museum collections or other sources, working with other individuals or organizations to exhibit loaned material of significance to Ty Cobb's life.

÷ Interpreting artifacts through its exhibition and education programs to enhance awareness, understanding and appreciation of Cobb's extraordinary accomplishments, both on and off the baseball field.

The present Ty Cobb Museum may be successful because of a failure to establish a memorial in the late 1960s and early 1970s.

In Charles C. Alexander's book, <u>Ty Cobb</u>, an ambitious scheme unfolded, not only to memorialize "the greatest and smartest player baseball has ever known" but also to attract tourists to the little town of Royston. "People who had known and liked Cobb and appreciated what he had done for the town had undertaken a project to commemorate the life of the man they understood to have been basically generous and warm-hearted," Alexander wrote, referring to the time shortly after Ty Cobb's death in 1961.

A group of prominent Royston citizens, led by Stewart Brown, Jr., started raising money to build a Ty Cobb museum shortly after Cobb's death. The group secured the passage of a bill in the Georgia legislature creating a "Ty Cobb Baseball Memorial Commission." The commission included such notables as Gov. Carl Sanders, former Gov. Ernest Vandiver, Mayor Ivan Allen of Atlanta, George Weiss, president of the New York Mets, and J. G. Taylor Spink, publisher of the *Sporting News*. Each biennium, the legislature was to make an appropriation for the project, and private contributions were to reach a half million dollars.

The site chosen for the memorial was two acres fronting U.S. Highway 29 on the western outskirts of Royston, just down the road from Cobb Memorial Hospital.

By 1970, the legislature had appropriated $175,000, but private contributions were far behind the projections with only about $20,000 collected. The largest single contribution of $2,500 had been made by John E. Fetzer, president of the Detroit Tigers.

The Commission did have enough money to build a structure made of brick with two wings and an open courtyard, but the lack of funds eventually forced cancellation of the original plan for a big bronze statue of Cobb to stand in the courtyard area.

Then, the group found that most Cobb baseball artifacts were not available; almost all of them had gone to the National Baseball Hall of Fame and Museum years earlier.

So, after 15 years of trying to provide a lasting monument to the most famous person ever to live in Royston, the Commission finally gave up on the project and deeded the property to the town, which made it into a new city hall. The small collection of Cobb memorabilia was moved over to the hospital.

While that first effort to recognize the successes of Ty Cobb, both on and off the field, was not a success, the current Museum in Royston is indeed successful. Visitors can learn much about "The Georgia Peach" and are able to purchase items from the museum's gift shop.

To commemorate the 50th anniversary of the Ty Cobb Educational Foundation, the Ty Cobb Museum unveiled a new exhibit during a 10:00 A.M. ceremony on October 4, 2003, and at the same time, released its third annual Ty Cobb Baseball Card.

The ceremony unveiling the Ty Cobb Educational Foundation exhibit was attended by members of the Foundation's Board of Trustees, their families, family members of Ty Cobb, and friends of the Museum.

Released at 12:00 noon on that day was a limited edition of 367 cards, released as a special tribute to the Educational Foundation that Ty Cobb started in late 1953, 50 years prior to the ceremony. Each card was numbered and sealed with the Ty Cobb Museum seal in an acrylic sleeve.

The professionally designed Ty Cobb Educational Foundation exhibit was a special feature of the Museum that had been planned for a number of years.

The inside entrance to the Ty Cobb Museum in Royston, Georgia.

Currently on display at The Ty Cobb Museum is a display of baseball bats, each signifying a major accomplishment of Ty Cobb and purchased at $1,000 each. Three noteworthy bats include: (left to right) 1936 - First player voted into the National Baseball Hall of Fame (donated by Mr. and Mrs. Michael S. Green); 1953 - Ty donates $100,000 to start Cobb Educational Foundation in honor of his father (donated by Dr. and Mrs. Frances J. Tedesco on behalf of the Ty Cobb Foundation); and 1999 - Sports Illustrated named Cobb as Georgia's Greatest Athlete of the 20th Century (donated by the Stewart Brown family).

An early photo of the Ty Cobb Memorial Hospital.

Pictured at the Ty Cobb Educational Foundation's 50th anniversary celebration on October 4, 2003, were members of the Foundation's Board of Trustees and their wives along with members of the Ty Cobb family. From left are LuAnn Tedesco, Mary Anne Murphy, Walter Y. Murphy, David Cobb, Peggy Cobb Schug, Frances J. Tedesco, Elna Lombard, Harry S. Downs, Mrs. Charlie Cobb, Melba Downs and Charlie Cobb. The Tedescos, Murphys, and Downs represented the Board of Trustees.

130